# Managing Product Design

# Managing Product Design

Mark Oakley

Weidenfeld and Nicolson
LONDON

First published in Great Britain by
George Weidenfeld & Nicolson Limited
91 Clapham High Street, London SW4 7TA

**British Library Cataloguing in Publication Data**

Oakley, Mark
    Managing product design.
    1. Design-Management
    I. Title
    745.4'068    NK1510
Copyright © 1984 by Mark Oakley

ISBN 0 297 78427 7 (cased)
ISBN 0 297 78442 0 (paper)

Filmset by Deltatype, Ellesmere Port
Printed in Great Britain by Butler & Tanner Ltd,
Frome and London

# Contents

# Acknowledgements

Some of the information presented in this book derives from a research project funded by the Science and Engineering Research Council. This support is gratefully acknowledged, as is the work done on the project by researcher Kul Pawar who conducted the field studies. Some material has appeared previously in the journals *Omega* (Pergamon) and *Design Studies* (Butterworths) and in the book *Operations Management in Practice*, edited by C D Lewis (Philip Allen). In each case, the permission and help of the publishers is appreciated.

During 1983, the author worked for the Council for National Academic Awards as Research Fellow on its Design Management Development Project. Although the book was substantially completed before the project started, this opportunity to examine design and management practice and education around the world has been of invaluable benefit whilst finalising the manuscript.

Finally, grateful thanks are extended to Jenny Hipkiss, Linda Harland and Maureen Wood for a splendid co-operative typing effort which enabled a tight deadline to be achieved.

# Foreword

The material in this book, which has been assembled over the last few years, reflects topics that are being taught and researched at the Aston Management Centre. The managerial aspects of product design have never received great attention, partly because most teaching in universities and colleges has been concerned with the technical aspects of design. It should be stressed at this point that this book is not intended to teach or examine basic design skills. There are plenty of books which give excellent information about designing mechanisms, or creating aesthetic forms or about design techniques in general. The issues examined in this book are those which confront managers who are responsible for the planning and organisation of design work. They may be design managers or general managers, or functional managers with primary responsibilities in areas such as production and marketing. They may work in firms where design is a continuous activity; on the other hand they may work for companies which tackle design projects only occasionally.

The basic reason why this book came to be written is very simple – the observation that too many British companies are failing to exploit product design. In many cases, foreign competitors are enjoying considerable market gains at the expense of British producers who often seem unable to drag their products out of the past.

Usually the problem is not a lack of design skills, but an inability to manage design. Frequently, companies rush into design exercises without any clear specification for their new product or a 'brief' to guide the project. They fail to look at their resources in order to assess what they can reasonably hope to achieve and they have little idea of what the market really wants. Even when a design project has reached a conclusion, managers may be at a loss to evaluate the results that have been achieved.

These comments may seem harsh and may even be dismissed as untrue by some. However, the recent trend in national import/export performance of manufactured goods makes the problem hard to deny – as does the experience of any perceptive purchaser of consumer products. The book is not intended to antagonise hard-pressed managers – it has been written to help them to tackle this design problem.

As well as practising managers, the book is intended to be of use to students who intend to become managers of one kind or another. Typically, it will be of interest to students on Master and Diploma in Business Administration type courses. Undergraduate students on management and engineering courses with up-to-date syllabuses are likely to find the book relevant to their studies as well. It is also hoped that it will be read by students at design schools who are interested in the wider aspects of their discipline. Much of the material which is presented has been used at Aston on various courses (including short, intensive courses for practising managers) and at other universities in the U.K. and overseas. As it has been used it has, of course, been tested and modified. Thousands of students have attended courses at Aston – one the largest business schools in Europe – and many of them have participated in design management courses.

The aim of the book is to introduce a range of topics which may arise in connection with design activities. It is not claimed that *all* possible topics have been included or even that the most important have been covered. As in other aspects of management studies, what is considered important by one individual may be discounted by another. Hence, the selection of material is a personal one, modified by experience in companies and classrooms. The author believes that the book has advantages over the few others that are available; for example, material is based on research as well as experience and particular attention has been paid to references for further reading which are often absent from books about design. However, the book *is* the result of a form of design exercise and, as such, it will conform to the First Law of Design which dictates that an end product is never perfect. It is left to the reader to decide what scope for improvement remains and suggestions will be graciously received – in the spirit of the Second Law of Design: the designer's solution may not be perfect, but it is always better than anyone else's!

Several case studies are included to illustrate the points being covered. There is nearly always a dilemma to be faced when preparing case studies from real life. To be most effective, real names and totally factual information should be used. Naturally, this usually includes some items of sensitive information which may cause embarrassment to those identified in the case. The case writer is then faced with the choice of writing either a bland case with apparent realism but limited content, or an explicit, informative case which disguises true identities and possibly alters some other data as well. The cases in this book fall into the latter category; all recount actual events.

Some of the material arises from a research project which has been examining elements of the working relationship between design and production departments in smaller, batch manufacturing companies. The reader will find that the design/production relationship is a topic which is prominent in the book; again this reflects the particular experience of the writer, who considers this to be the most important of all the working relationships between design and the other functions in an enterprise.

# 1 Design and Design Management

## 1.1 Why Design?

Design as a resource is frequently misunderstood and misused by both managers and companies. The main purpose of this chapter is to discuss the nature of design activity and the different manifestations of design but first, to justify the opening sentence, consider the following:

The need for high productivity in industry is widely acknowledged. Rarely a day passes without a reference being made by a politician or industrialist to the necessity for goods to be produced as cheaply as possible in order to compete with foreign firms. Almost always, these people talk about increased productivity solely in terms of better factory organisation, removal of restrictive labour practices and, often rather crudely, getting people to work harder or for longer periods. At the time of writing this book, a major British company was plunged into a lengthy strike because of the determination of its management to improve competitiveness and productivity by eliminating a 3–minute washing allowance at the end of each working shift. By whatever means that company used to measure productivity, the hoped-for result could only have been an improvement of the order of a fraction of one percent at best.

Compare that with the experience of another company, a major European manufacturer of colour television receivers. *Figure 1.1* shows the dramatic reduction in labour content achieved over a 15 year period. The reduction was almost entirely brought about by consistent and relentless attention to the design of the product. As new processes and technologies were developed, these were adopted with the result that the labour content was reduced by more that two-thirds during the 15 years. Despite increases in material, fuel and labour costs (the hourly rate for the latter by some 3 times), the company was still able to reduce the overall manufacturing cost by 20%.

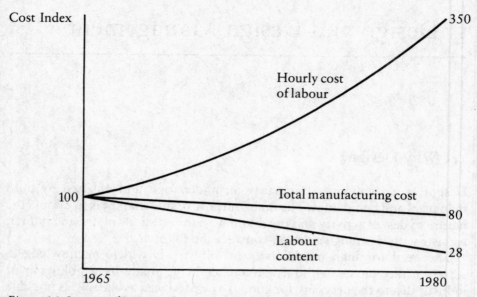

*Figure 1.1  Impact of Design Changes on Manufacturing Cost of Colour Television Receivers*

This example supports the case, made by one expert on design management, for the effect of design inputs to a company to be expressed through conventional financial ratios.[1] He believes that the impact of design is best demonstrated by means of quantitative measures that enable managers to approach design through the 'language' of business. In this way, with qualitative data in support (but not as a sole means of assessment) managers are more easily able to justify to themselves and their colleagues expenditure on design resources. So, design for productivity is just one aspect which managers may not exploit to the full. Another is what might be called design for consumer appeal – it is sometimes remarked that many British goods lack the flair, style and attractiveness which characterise products made in other countries. This is despite the general acknowledgement that British design education and British designers are second to none as highlighted by the fact that the chief designers of many companies around the world are British.

The problem must lie in the management of the design function. Whether it is because British managers believe that the appearance of their product is unimportant or whether it is because they do think it important but that no special skill is required to achieve the necessary standards (or even because they are simply frightened or suspicious of designers) the fact remains that it is a management problem and management must bear the responsibility for solving it. A notable feature of British companies – compared with German and Japanese[2,3,4] companies in particular – is the frequent lack of representation of the design function at board level. Considering the critical role played by design this is a depressing state of affairs made even worse in those numerous manufacturing companies which also have insufficient or non-existent technical expertise at the top level. No doubt, the roots of this problem can be traced back through our cultural and educational systems – the recent discovery by the writer that classics is still the largest single department at one of our best-known public schools, might indicate little hope for future change – but it is not the purpose of this book to crusade for managerial or social revolution. Rather, the intention is simply to give some information about managing design that may be followed by managers at all levels.

During the last few years a number of reports[5,6,7] have examined the problems surrounding design practice and education in the United Kingdom. Whilst each has had an impact upon some of the problems that were being addressed, none has been able to generate the level of concern that is required to make any widespread improvement in the status and exploitation of design. However, there are currently signs of an emerging awareness that industrial success is now very closely dependent upon design performance. In past decades, the key problems that had to be solved by the producers of goods were, successively, achieving quantity (meeting post-war demand), then quality, then diversity. Today, the purchasers of most products are able to choose between many competing models all offering similar quality and value for money. Increasingly, design is the factor which determines the final purchase decision.

At this stage, it might seem useful to try to give some kind of definition of design; after all, that is the conventional thing to do at this point in a book. Unfortunately, definitions are often difficult to formulate or misleading to adopt and never more so than in this case; the term 'design' is in common use but in many different contexts. Reference to one well-known book on design methodology[8] reveals a considerable number of diverse definitions drawn from a range of sources. Rather than choose one, or try to combine several, it is more sensible at this stage to allow the reader to reflect on his or her own personal definitions of 'design' in general and 'product design' in particular. As progress is made through the book, it is intended that the nature and content of product design will become clear without the need to start with an explicit definition. In other words, the book's main purpose is to explain the subject, and to highlight the key problem areas.

## 1.2 Product Design in Context

For a number of reasons, this book is concerned primarily with managing the design of products rather than managing all aspects of design. First, it is the one aspect of design of which most managers are likely to have some experience and knowledge. Second, research and experience shows it to be an area in which considerable management problems exist.[9,10,11] Finally, it is an area of design activity most likely to be tackled on a 'do-it-yourself' basis; most companies seek expert advice as a matter of course on the design of promotional material or the design of new premises, but many use no outside help at all when designing products. However, having said that, it is important to bear in mind that not only are other kinds of design important in companies but also that there are significant relationships between product design and these other kinds. In most companies the following design activities will be found in addition to product design:

**Packaging Design.** All products must be transported to the customer in some kind of container. At one extreme, potatoes may be most conveniently packaged in a simple paper sack, while at the other, a delicate medical product may require the protection of an ingenious package more expensive than the product itself. In between these extremes, there are thousands of different forms of packaging, the design of which is, in many cases, at least as important in influencing consumer decision as the design of the product which they contain. As well as the choice of the material for a package (plastic, paper, glass, metal etc.) it is also necessary to decide the shape, colour, decoration and lettering. This aspect is generally referred to as:

**Graphic Design.** Specialists in graphic design may be concerned with many types of projects such as the layout of brochures and company stationery, as well as the appearance of product packages. Whilst, as in most forms of design work, a considerable element of 'flair' is required, the world of the graphic designer demands a good understanding of basic principles. When it is appropriate to use upper and/or lower case type, what 'messages' different shapes and colours can convey to viewers, how to 'balance' the layout of printed material – these are all examples of the skills that are part of graphic design.

**Building Design**, both interior and exterior, is another specialisation. For most businesses the days are long gone when the appearance and layout of their premises could be left to the whim of a local contractor. The expectations of customers or users are such that the design of the building may be viewed at least as critically as the product or service which it contains. The design of a public house is a good example of how building design may have a far greater influence on the sale of the basic product (ie. the beer, food, etc.) than the actual design of that product. Similarly, sales of petrol (which most people would consider to be a standard product regardless of the company which produces it) depend strongly on the image of the company as presented through the design of its filling stations.

**Exhibition design** brings together both graphic design and building (interior) design but is really a specialisation in its own right. The problems of creating an impact in a confined space, when many other companies may be trying to do the same thing, requires skill and experience in graphics, lighting, perspectives and audio systems.

Many other varieties of design may be encountered although these can usually be included in the categories already discussed. For example, fashion and textile design as a form of product design, store design as a division of interior design, and so on. In many companies, what may be said to link all these aspects of design is the concept of:

**Corporate identity.** It is often desirable that all the different manifestations of design should be related to each other and should contribute to the presentation of a uniform image of the company to customers, suppliers and other groups. In companies with a strong corporate identity, the products or services, buildings, publicity material and stationery may all have common characteristics such as the use of a standard 'house-style' typeface, standard colour schemes and distinctive shapes or forms. *Figure* 1.2 helps to explain what can be achieved through a corporate identity

**1** Every corporation has a corporate image in the minds of the people who are aware of it.

**2** There are different ideas about the corporation in the minds of different people.

**3** The appearance of any corporation is made up of several areas: advertising, architecture, packaging, products, promotion, publications, stationery, transport, uniforms, etc.

**4** A consistent and organised control of each area constitutes design management.

**5** Design coordination relates the different areas in order to produce a consistent identification system throughout the corporation.

**6** Through proper control and coordination, all visual manifestations of a corporation are seen to come from the same source. All new activities and products benefit from already-invested goodwill, each area reinforcing and complementing all other areas.

**7** A strong image clarifies the interface between corporation and public. It helps to make clear to shareholders what they own and strengthens the interface between corporation and financial circles.

**8** A strong corporate image also clarifies and emphasises the interface between corporation and staff.

**9** In the absence of design management and coordination these interfaces between corporation and public, and between corporation and staff, will be blurred.

**10** When a number of different companies within an organisation should be seen to belong to one group, their sub-identities should form part of the overall identity.

**11** Shareholders, banks and finance must have a clear idea of the corporation in order to support it.

**12** Staff recruitment becomes, for large corporations, a crucial activity, and a favourable image of the corporation must increase interest and motivate potential job applicants.

Based on a design by Henrion, Ludlow and Schmidt, Consultant Designers, London.

*Figure 1.2 Advantages of a Corporate Identity Programme*

programme, a consequence of which is often the compilation of some kind of design manual to promote the use of preferred design forms. The main reason for stressing here the importance of corporate identity and the various specialisms of design, is to avoid the danger of presenting a too narrow view of product design. In many different fields today, a good product alone is not sufficient to ensure a successful business. The computer industry has long recognised this; the basic product design must be right but so must be the service, supplies and information systems which support the product. Customers need to be reassured that the equipment which they buy or rent (but about which they probably have little understanding) is part of a reliable and confident operation. The main way that this reassurance is given is by demonstrating a considerate and logical business approach; the key to this is integrated, appropriate design which links the product firmly with the company that supplies it.

Even in much less sophisticated areas, the customer may need to be given the confidence to buy a particular brand of a product – a bar of soap may need to do much more than help remove dirt for example. In such a case there may be a limit to the information that can be conveyed by the product itself about the functions it performs, so its design must be integrated with the other forms of design used by the company.

## 1.3 The Scope of Design Management

This book considers product design in the broadest sense. It is not concerned just with the basic activities of designing – sketching, testing, perfecting and handing over to production – but with the complete process involved in moving from the point where a newly designed product is successfully introduced into the manufacturing system and the market. The total design process involves at least three phases of activity:

**Formulation.** Before any technical design work can be carried out, a 'specification' or 'brief' must be prepared which will set the limits and requirements of the product. The formulation of the specification must be done in the light of opportunities in markets and in the company itself. This means that following a realisation that some problem exists and that design effort is required, a critical analysis is required of markets, the company and the general environment within which it operates. These issues are discussed in the following chapter.

**Evolution.** The activities mentioned in the first paragraph of this section take place within the evolution phase. For the design manager, the main consideration will be the effective organisation of these activities; this will be examined in chapters 6 and 7.

**Transfer.** Once an effective design has been achieved in the design department, there remains the problem of successfully transferring it to the production system and from there to the customer. This is a critical aspect of design management which will be discussed in several of the chapters and case studies.

Of all the decisions taken by managers, those concerning the design of new products and improved products often have the most dramatic effect on the general success of the enterprise. A new idea for a product which is soundly conceived, expertly designed, efficiently introduced into the production system, and successfully presented to the market will enhance the profitability and growth prospects of the firm. Conversely, a decision about a new product which is taken without enthusiasm or a real understanding of the issues involved, followed by a mis-directed design programme and a badly handled transfer to production is, sadly, the all-too-common hallmark of the poorly managed company.

Control of the tasks associated with design should be an essential part of general management. But a great many problems stem from the fact that in important respects these tasks are quite different from those found in the dominant activity of most manufacturing firms – namely, production. For example, production managers aim to achieve continuity of output by using fairly precise methods of scheduling and control. Product design programmes cannot be organised in the same manner. The predictability and standardisation found in well-planned production systems are not present to the same degree in new product programmes where often the predominant features seem to be uncertainty and diversity. Perhaps it is because of these problems that many firms attempt a complete separation of production and design activities. This is rarely successful unless communications are exceptionally good and there is a well developed procedure for the smooth handover of new products from design to production. For the majority of firms, new product activities must be an integral part of the general system of operation. All managers, whether line or staff, specialist or generalist, must expect new product decisions and responsibilites to be a normal part of their work. As with other business activities, management responsibilities for design can be examined at two levels: at a higher, policy-making level and at the project or operating level. Several recent analyses have been made of the problems at both levels – that of Topalian[9] is a useful and typical example – and the following two sections present a summary of the key issues, most of which are covered in further detail in later chapters. ¶ — *conclude*

## 1.4 Design Policy Management

This is a prime responsibility of the board of every company – although as noted earlier, a common absence of design and technical knowledge may well undermine the quality of the decisions which have to be made. Determining the general design policy is the overall task:- Will the company be a design leader or follower? How will product appearance rank against other characteristics such as quality, delivery performance, manufacturability or selling price? Does the market for the product experience violent fluctuations in design or a steady evolution of design? In order to formulate design policy, a good understanding is required of both the nature of the market and the design potential of the product. A good example of effective design policy making was featured in a recent article in the Financial Times newspaper.[12] The article examined one carpet company based in Kidderminster, the traditional centre of the British carpet industry. Against the trend of bankruptcies caused by over-capacity and foreign competition, this company was enjoying growth and healthy profitability. The chairman, who had transferred the once-ailing company's fortunes, unequivocally put its new success down to having an appropriate design policy. On joining the company, one of his first actions had been to commission market research to discover what motivated customers when they purchased carpets. From this research he was able to distil the following priority of requirements:

– Colour
– Pattern
– Construction
– Performance
– Price

So dominant was the issue of colours and patterns, that the company made this a top priority. Experiments were conducted to determine what range of design configurations were possible using the equipment the company had available. Other aspects of design policy, for example, point-of-sale material and vehicle livery — were also reviewed so that an appropriate company image could be developed. Product quality and delivery performance were given a high priority as well because these factors were important to retailers who were reluctant to recommend troublesome products.

Some readers might object that this is hardly a typical example since it is obvious that aesthetic design must be a major consideration in the purchase of carpets. That may be true but the fact remains that, whether they understood the point or not, most other carpet manufacturers did not have a design policy which enabled them to fully exploit their markets in the systematic way that this company had done. Of those still in business, many were still producing colour ranges and 'car smash' patterns that may have satisfied customers 15 years earlier, but no longer suited current tastes and furnishing trends. To some degree, exactly the same arguments apply to every single product offered for sale — from the humblest ball point pen to the most advanced piece of electronic equipment. Moving from this example of the carpet manufacturer, further elements of design policy management can be listed in more detail:

## Setting design objectives
Deciding the role that design should and can play in the company's activities. In order to do this it is necessary to find out what weight is given by the customer to design features compared with other aspects. Also the company must decide whether it wishes to satisfy many different design tastes or to concentrate on a single area. Many examples of this may be seen in the motor industry. Some companies pursue design solutions which embody 'safety', others seek to consistently emphasise 'sportiness' or 'reliability'. One manufacturer's vehicles may actually be no more 'safe' or 'reliable' than another's; but the skill of the designer may give the suggestion that it is — if that is one of the design objectives of the company. Sometimes the large motor manufacturers may produce many variants of a single model which attempt to satisfy, not always successfully, a wide range

of desires; spoilers and air dams may be added to give sports appeal, walnut facias and leather seats to create an atmosphere of nostalgia or electronic gadgets and accessories to satisfy the 'executive' taste.

## Defining, setting and maintaining design standards

This is rather different from design objectives which are about *what* a company wants to achieve. Design standards relate to *how* the results will be achieved. Top management must decide which areas of excellence it wishes to develop. Does it wish to be a leader in aesthetics and win prizes for styling or finish? Does it want to emphasise technical performance? Or ergonomics? Or value for money? These standards must be set out in a form which is meaningful; it is no good dismissing these issues, like one chairman of a major company by saying 'my people know I won't take second-best'. Second-best to him might be third or fourth-best to another chairman. Who knows?

Standards should be defined in quantitative terms where possible. For example, technical performance in terms of acceptable failure rate, overload capacity, working life – whatever are the relevant characteristics for each product. Aspects of aesthetic design may be more difficult to quantify, but an attempt should still be made. Accumulations of design awards *may* be a useful indication but consistent high marks over other manufacturers in consumer preference tests might be much better.

Maintaining design standards is also a top management responsibility, just like maintaining financial or legal standards. The best way to do this is to compile a design manual which not only sets out the standards but may include examples of preferred colours, lettering styles, material applications, process settings, etc. In some cases, it may be appropriate to include other information in the design manual such as guidelines for recruiting consultant designers, or details of relevant national and international standards. On this latter point, an important recent report[13] emphasises the desirability that products should be more widely certified against reputable and recognised standards as a means of indicating excellence in design and quality to purchasers, especially those overseas. The report advocates that more schemes should be set up to encourage certification and approval. Even in the absence of compulsion, companies would be well advised to consider the benefits of aiming to meet or exceed official standards as well as their own. It is noticeable how common it is for goods on sale on the

Continent to stress compliance with one or more officially recognised standards.

## Audits of design

Associated with the topic of design standards is the question of whether the company has the resources – or knows how to use the resources – necessary to achieve the standards which have been set. From time to time, senior management must review design activities to ensure that design objectives and standards are being maintained. The idea of a design audit may seem distasteful to some managers but there is no reason why this should be so. Providing the purpose of the audit is made clear – to check out design directions, resources and results, rather than personal effort or perform-ance – there should be no adverse reaction. Indeed this is a task which should be carried out jointly by top management and staff at the project level. Osola[14] recommends on the basis of his experience that knowledge-able outsiders should also be involved in the process, on the grounds that the insiders may lack objectivity or breath of information. Situations may be envisaged where this would not be practical (perhaps for security reasons) although this might be an ideal activity in which to involve non-executive directors. The essential requirement is that the following basic questions are tackled:

What design skills are available to the company?
What design management skills are available?
What use has been made of design resources during the review period?
What design results have been achieved compared with competitors?
What are the weaknesses and strengths of design in the company?
Is the company setting appropriate standards for design?
Is the company setting appropriate objectives for design?

## Organisation for design activity

Under this heading come several related issues. First, the question of the focus of responsibility for design at the top level of companies will be considered more precisely. In the last few pages, this problem has been dodged by simply talking about 'board level responsibility'. But now the question should be raised about what this means in practice. Very few companies have a director of design as a member of the board. Usually the responsibility for design is combined with that for some other function, typically marketing, production or research and development. Sometimes, design matters are the responsibility of no single individual and are either considered by the board as a whole – or not consciously considered at all.

The arguments for and against directors of design are voiced periodically in the design press – not apparently in the management press, though. The main argument in favour of design directors is that they increase the chances that design will receive equal attention alongside all the other considerations before a board. Also, when necessary, there is a 'champion' at the top level of the company to press for continued support for projects that may be in danger of losing favour for no good reason. With a specific individual assigned to design, there is a much better chance that the design policy issues will actually receive the necessary thought and action.

Against this is the view that design directors may 'institutionalise' design – decisions *will* be taken, but they will tend towards the humdrum and safe; instead of innovation, predictability will dominate. Examples may be quoted of companies which have employed well known designers as directors and have enjoyed success in the medium term only to find that the passage of time has turned their distinctive products into liabilities as they were overtaken by other companies with more flexible design attitudes. Added to this may be the danger that a design director wishes to build up his department and increase his span of control; in doing this he may eliminate the use of outside designers or limit the freedom of his own staff to develop wider working relationships.

On balance, given the present lack of design expertise and involvement at the top level of so many British companies, it is probably best to advocate, at a minimum, the allocation of responsibility for design matters to a named director. Companies whose existing directors do not possess sufficient knowledge to take on this task should consider making an additional appointment as early as possible. To leave design as a general responsibility of the board, may put the topic at the level of importance of say, plant maintenance or staff training – both necessary but neither likely to have the same influence on the overall success of the company as design and design policy making.

Having discussed the question of board level representation, the next organisational issue to be tackled is the balance between design activity inside and outside the company. Not every company has, or needs, a fully-fledged design department. For some firms, providing there is an individual

who understands the design problems that require attention, it may be quite satisfactory to sub-contract all design activities. In this case, all stages in the design process right up to and including the preparation of final manufacturing drawings, may be handed over to a specialist outside unit. As a general rule, it is appropriate to use outside design units when:
— Internal resources are absent or fully occupied *or*
— A rapid result is needed which internal resources alone could not provide *or*
— Specialist skills are required which would be uneconomic to recruit specially for a single project *and*
— Adequate management capacity is available to coordinate the external work.

Of course, some projects may be based partly internally and partly externally. As a general rule, companies which are in areas of business where fashion changes are frequent, or technology is evolving rapidly, should have strong internal design departments, otherwise basic product knowledge will be absent from the company. Where fashion and technology have little influence, outside design work can be highly useful in exploiting 'new angles'. All firms must be aware of the danger of a 'too isolated' attitude about design work – outsiders are often highly important in identifying design problems or weaknesses. However, as will be discussed in chapter 9 these 'outsiders' may be found within the company and even if not already experienced in design methods, may be able to make a significant contribution to the design process.

Because the organisation of design departments and their position in the structure of the firm are such important issues, most of chapter 4 is devoted to the topic. After the setting of design objectives, decisions about organising for design within the firm are the most important aspects of design policy making.

## Evaluation of design results

The final major element of design policy is that relating to the evaluation of design. Put simply, for each design exercise the question must be asked 'does the result satisfy the original objectives?' This question may be difficult to answer because it requires that an assessment is made for both the design process and of the product which has been designed. How is this to be done by managers who may have little confidence in their own assessment of aesthetic or functional aspects of products? Although difficult, the problem can be tackled at board level by developing guidelines to direct the evaluation process.

## 1.5 Design Project Management

When a range of design projects was examined by the writer and a research colleague[11] it was clear that many of the problems which arose were similar in nature to those in non-design areas of companies. Further, managing design projects involves the use of many skills and techniques familiar to managers of all kinds. Thus, any manager responsible for design activities, will find his traditional skills in full use (although probably in unfamiliar situations). However, a number of activities are unique to design work and several others have special considerations associated with them. In order to examine these activities fully, a model of the design process will now be developed, followed by brief comments in this section on the main issues and detailed analyses in later chapters of the key problem areas.

There are always dangers in attempting to present a 'typical' model of any human activity, and designing is no exception. However, in order to have some common ground between reader and writer, a basic model is proposed with the following constraints borne in mind:

- The concern is with product design rather than other forms of design such as those discussed earlier in this chapter.
- Quantity production is being considered rather than unit production (but not necessarily mass production).
- The design activity is predominantly in-house rather than entirely contracted out.

Even within these limits, a standardised model may be misleading; Jones[8] discusses thirty-seven different design methodologies some of which would require fundamental alteration of the basic model. The basis of a model has been indicated already at the beginning of section 1.3, and this is shown in *figure 1.3*.

The first point to note is that the linear form of this model is unsatisfactory. If perfection in design achievement were a possibility the

model might be of use as it stands; but designs are never perfect and even if
they were, restless markets would soon render them inadequate. Hence,
design must be viewed as a circular process – or more realistically as a spiral
process if we wish to stress that design is an evolving activity. Also missing
from the basic linear model is any indication of the reaction of the market to
the design result. The basic model can now be refined as shown in *figure 1.4*.
It will be noticed that the model has been drawn in the form of a

Formulation of
problem ————————→ Evolution of
solution ————————→ Transfer of results
to production and
the market

*Figure 1.3   An Elementary Linear Model of the Product Design Process*

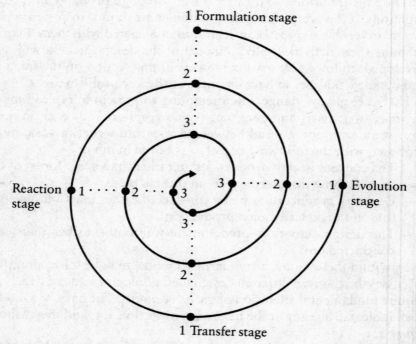

*Figure 1.4   A Spiral Model of the Product Design Process*

converging spiral. This emphasises two points. First, as each cycle is traversed, more knowledge should be gained as familar ground is explored. This will lead to quicker, more efficient design activity as a general rule. Occasionally, major discontinuities will be encountered which could be envisaged as precipitating shifts to spirals of different dimensions. Second, this spiral form also underlines the point that new technology is forcing the different activities closer together. Computer aided design (CAD) equipment linked with computer controlled manufacturing processes can already combine much of the 'evolution' phase with much of the 'transfer' phase. Ultimately, technology will permit some very rapid design processes which will have far reaching consequences for all of us. Extreme product diversity will be possible allowing individual consumers needs to be satisfied precisely; the era of uniform mass production will have come to a close. In order to expand this basic model the main components of the four activities can be identified as:

— **Formulation:** problem investigation
problem definition
product specification
design brief

— **Evolution:** idea generation
solution refinement
prototype development
design freeze

— **Transfer:** manufacturing drawings/data compilation
process modification finalised
start up tests
full scale production
delivery of new product to customer

— **Reaction:** customer appraisal
after-sales service activities
problem investigation

These component parts of the design process will be examined at various points in the book; the case studies are important in this respect because they illustrate better than theoretical discussion the problems which actually arise in practice. The amount of coverage in each case has been determined by the writer's judgement of which are the key problem areas. So, for example, much discussion is presented on project briefs and specifications; rather less on starting up the manufacture of new products. For the design manager, there are a number of additional responsibilities which must receive attention during each project cycle:

- Planning, costing and administration of design projects
- Recruiting designers and other specialists
- Managing project groups
- Attending to legal aspects of design
- Evaluating each project on completion.

## 1.6 Conclusion

The aim of this chapter has been to give an indication of the scope of the book as a whole. First, a case was made for the importance of product design within the company — no matter how efficient a firm's manufacturing and distribution systems may be, no long term success can be achieved unless the product is of a high standard, uses the most up-to-date technology and satisfies the desires of the customer. Next, the nature of design management was discussed together with the question of where in the company hierarchy this responsibility should rest. The opinion was emphatically expressed that responsibility must lie at the top level — but the continuing problem was recognised of a general lack of design skills and knowledge at this level in British companies. It is the basic aim of this book to help ameliorate this situation and the final section of the chapter concentrated upon giving an outline of the key management tasks at both the policy-management (board) level and at the project level. These topics will be examined in greater detail in the remainder of the book.

# 2 Decisions about New Products

## 2.1 Introduction

Before any design work can begin, it is necessary to decide the real needs of the company. Too often, firms rush into expensive design projects without a clear understanding of what they are doing and what they may be able to achieve. Some of the case studies in this book illustrate the problem.

To manage design effectively, it is essential that new or improved products are allowed to appear only after careful planning has confirmed a need for them. This planning must start with a dispassionate assessment of the company's skills and resources, together with detailed information about markets, both as they are now and as they are expected to be in the future. Designers can have an important role to play in this work.

## 2.2 The Need to Design New or Better Products

All firms which desire to grow and prosper must give top priority to developing a product strategy. Even those companies content to maintain just a constant level of turnover and profits cannot escape the need to plan for new products. No matter how well-established a firm may be, products which are successful now might be struggling in their markets in a few years time. Unless replacements or improvements have been planned and developed, crisis action may well be the result. Crash programmes to provide new products do not stand a very good chance of success – money is short, time is very short, and tempers tend to be extremely short. Managers and designers must work together to be aware of the threats which may undermine their existing products. Early identification of danger signals gives the best chance of planning to meet the impending challenge. Broadly, these threats may be classified under five headings:

### Competition from within the industry

This is relatively easy to monitor. Employees change firms and constitute a flow of information and expertise. Trade journals report on new developments and manufacturers' associations publish data on trends in member companies. Consultant designers from outside the company may make a particularly valuable contribution for their professional activities and involvement in different projects can give them unique knowledge about industrial trends at home and abroad. Frequently, companies may use designers extensively at the project stage, but overlook the potentially greater benefits that may be achieved by their involvement at the planning stage as well.

### Competition from outside the industry

This is much more of a problem than threats from within the industry. Issues of new technology are frequently involved which only companies with wide resources can hope to counteract. Sometimes whole industries are jeopardised by failure to detect and react to outside advances. In recent times, probably the most famous example has been the failure of the mechanical watch industry to meet the challenge of electronics. The world's major supplier of mechanical watches, Switzerland, was lulled by decades of market domination and completely failed to match the challenge of the new technology because warning signs were not seen and acted upon early enough.[1] The impact upon market share, employment and turnover was dramatic; survival was achieved only by means of radical measures which included acquiring from competitors the rights to use the new technology and reformulating product strategy. Previously the Swiss had stressed reliability and accuracy – now these qualities were available to an even higher degree in the cheapest of electronic watches. The new strategy concentrated upon design, style and fashion to a much greater extent than before.

A less dramatic example was the introduction some years ago by the Moulton Company of the small wheeled bicycle which featured a number of novel design features including rubber suspension.[2] The traditional manufacturers found themselves with obsolete designs and had to move quickly to follow the new trend imposed on their business from outside.

**Changes of attitude, fashion and taste**
These may occur gradually – for example, the substitution of convenience foods for fresh foods – or abruptly as in the case of some types and styles of clothing. In either case, managers need to consider the implications for their firms and to develop new products accordingly. Again, it is the designers who are likely to have the most up-to-date knowledge of these trends. Together with reliable market research data, their views should be carefully considered each time the product plan is reviewed.

**Legal changes and political trends**
Changes of a legal nature are usually evident long before they actually happen. For example, tobacco manufacturers have had plenty of time to diversify into new product areas ahead of restrictions on the sale of their traditional products. Political changes and their impact may be more of a problem. Obviously, in some industries a change in national or inter-national political orientation may have a direct effect – for example, aerospace companies may be forced to review the balance of their military and civil programmes. It is debatable whether political swings may have more general, subtle effects on product designs and strategies.

**Diminishing natural resources**
This has been the subject of much discussion and speculation but there is ample evidence that many products will need to change considerably.[3] Vehicles will be designed to consume less fuel and will be constructed using smaller quantities of steel and other materials. New forms of packaging for goods will be introduced as some materials become scarce. Many traditional products will disappear. The challenges for product designers may be considerable, but there will be many opportunities as well as threats. Already we see new scope for the manufacturers of insulation products and for companies which can design 'energy efficient' versions of traditional products, ranging from motor cars to kitchen gadgets.

Whilst the 'information technology revolution' has been set on its way by discoveries in science and engineering, its continued progress and, the design opportunities which it creates, depends in part on the availability and cost of natural resources. Manual and mechanical methods will be replaced more readily where substantial savings of expensive resources can be achieved. Diverse examples include: centralised banking and accounting systems; introduction of condition monitoring of equipment in place of regular component replacement; reduction of safety stocks and lead times through the use of more sophisticated inventory control systems. It is the author's observation that designers raise these issues and discuss them more readily and knowledgeably than managers or businessmen, who tend to be concerned with more immediate problems. Similarly, designers more frequently express concern about long-term personal or group objectives – a sense of 'mission' about their work. No doubt, this reflects differences in training and experience but it underlines the value of the contribution that designers can make to the planning process.

Sooner or later, all firms experience influences which may be categorised under one or more of the preceding five headings. Established products have to be redesigned or replaced as a result. In new firms the same problems are likely to be encountered, but there are two special features of such firms which reinforce the need for new products.

- Many new firms are based on a single product idea. This implies vulnerability to competitive threats and for security additional products must be developed as quickly as possible.
- Frequently, new firms are under-capitalised and in order to survive must build up income levels swiftly. Additional new products which can be accommodated in the existing operations system can generate this income.

## 2.3 The Product Life-Cycle Concept

The last section presented a number of reasons to support the view that no firm can expect to escape for ever the need to modify or replace its products. Notwithstanding this, it is true that there are many products which have always been necessary and which will be sought indefinitely, for example bread, shoes and medical drugs. However, within these broad classifications, major and minor variations are always occurring. Particular forms of products always have finite lives in terms of their value to the company as part of its operations. The example of men's shoes illustrates this point. For many years, the standard construction consisted of leather for both the upper and the sole. The introduction of rubber soles caused a decline in the demand for all-leather products because of the better wearing properties of rubber. Later, polyurethane and other plastic materials became available and another switch in demand resulted. These changes in materials were accompanied by important changes in methods of manufacture, such as assembly by means of adhesives rather than traditional stitching. Individual firms in the industry found they had to change product designs and manufacturing processes or go out of business.

This concept of limited product life is well known to marketing specialists but, sometimes, is less well appreciated by other managers. The plotting of *life-cycle curves* helps to demonstrate several important points:
- The life of a product design is never infinite;
- Adequate indication is usually available that revised or new designs are needed;
- Failure to develop and launch new products in time may result in a temporary decline in profitability or even the death of the enterprise.

A generalised life-cycle is shown in *figure 2.1*. It is usual to relate sales volume to time, but records of production output against time could also provide similar information assuming that any additional supplies of the

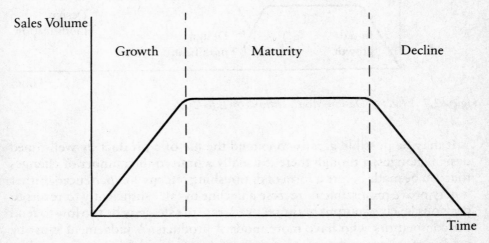

*Figure 2.1 Typical Form of Product Life-Cycle Curve*

product obtained by the company from elsewhere are included in the calculations.

The form of the life-cycle curve will be different for every product. Some products have a rapid growth in sales and then decline almost immediately. Other products continue to exhibit a rising trend even during the 'mature' period followed by a gradual or sudden decline.

Often a decline in sales can be be reversed by modifying the design of the product – a 'facelift' or a technical alteration to allow some new element of technology to be introduced. The effect of such actions may be to change the form of the life cycle plot along the lines of *figure* 2.2.

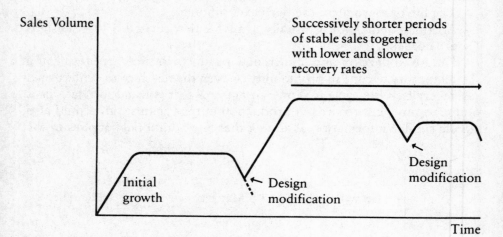

Figure 2.2  *Effect of Design Modifications on Life-Cycle*

It may be possible greatly to extend the life of a product by well-timed design changes, although there is usually a limit to the number of changes that can be made before a form of diminishing returns is experienced. Either it may prove impossible to reverse a decline in sales sufficiently to revert to previous levels of output or the recovery rate of sales may be too low to fend off competitors who have more modern products. A judgement must be made about the cost/benefit comparison between modifying an old product relatively cheaply as just described or investing more heavily in a completely new product form. Unfortunately, too many companies opt for the cheap modification to an existing product when market circumstances actually demand a new design and would reward the effort by providing much higher turnover. However, when it is decided that it is appropriate to introduce a totally new product, it is important that this should be done before the decline in sales of the original product has advanced too far. This

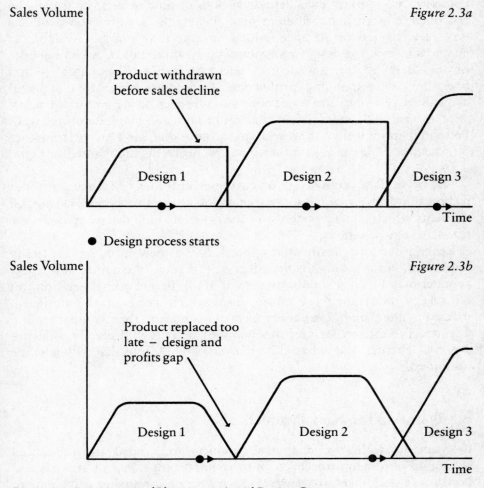

Figure 2.3  Importance of Planning to Avoid Design Gaps

is particularly important in firms which are based on a small number of products. Firms which provide a broad range of different products are less vulnerable, but still need to ensure that sufficient new products are being developed to provide continuity of turnover and profits.

The basic problem associated with the design and development of new products is that the process, in addition to money and management commitment, requires considerable periods of time, which can usually be reckoned in months and often in years. Unless the need for new products is perceived well in advance, sufficient time may not be available to enable a competent design programme to be undertaken. A consequence of this may be the unwelcome emergence of a 'design gap' – and probably a corresponding 'profits gap'. Companies which are competent at product planning aim to develop an approach to design and product strategy that will avoid violent changes in sales and manufacturing levels. Presented graphically, they seek to achieve the kind of performance represented in *figure 2.3a* rather than the problems highlighted in *figure 2.3b*.

Life-cycle data, knowledge of customer attitudes, information about technical advances and an awareness of competitors' actions are all elements which managers need to consider in making decisions about the timing of new products.

Recognising the forthcoming need for a new product is vitally important, but it is only the first step. At this stage, the nature of the new product may be known only vaguely, if at all. Before a final decision can be taken about the type of product which needs to be designed, managers must analyse a variety of features both in their companies and outside. The effectiveness of this planning activity will greatly influence eventual success and what this analysis should consider will now be examined.

## 2.4 Planning for New Products

Between the realisation that new products are needed and the actual setting up of design projects come three important stages of analysis and decision. These stages are represented in *figure 2.4* together with some of the main points of consideration and constraint.

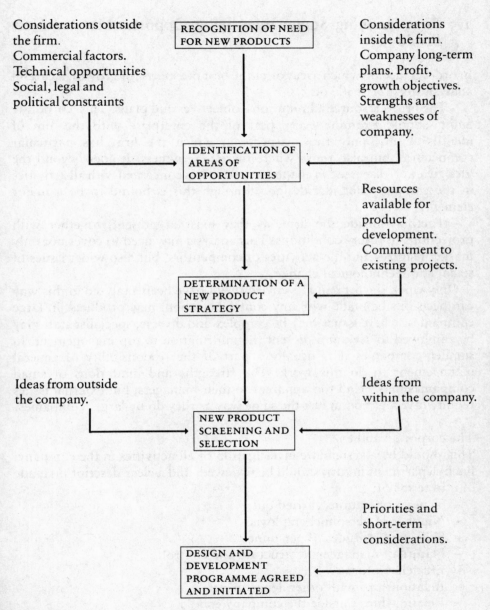

Considerations outside the firm.
Commercial factors.
Technical opportunities
Social, legal and political constraints

RECOGNITION OF NEED FOR NEW PRODUCTS

Considerations inside the firm. Company long-term plans. Profit, growth objectives. Strengths and weaknesses of company.

IDENTIFICATION OF AREAS OF OPPORTUNITIES

Resources available for product development. Commitment to existing projects.

DETERMINATION OF A NEW PRODUCT STRATEGY

Ideas from outside the company.

NEW PRODUCT SCREENING AND SELECTION

Ideas from within the company.

Priorities and short-term considerations.

DESIGN AND DEVELOPMENT PROGRAMME AGREED AND INITIATED

*Figure 2.4  A Decision Plan for New Products*

## 2.5 First Planning Stage: Identifying Opportunities for New Products

In order to decide which areas offer the best prospects for growth, a careful analysis must be made of:

– The firm's resources, limitations, objectives and plans. This 'corporate audit' should examine every part of the enterprise with the aim of identifying not only those aspects in which the firm has particular competence, but also those where there is weakness. It goes beyond the 'design audit' discussed in chapter 1, in that it is concerned with all activities in the company not just design, although this is bound to be a major element.

– Factors outside the firm, as they exist at present, together with projections of future conditions. This analysis may need to cover not only market features and the activities of competitors, but also wider issues of social and technological change.

Only when the firm and its environment have been analysed in this way can decisions be made with any confidence about new products. In large companies, where issues may be complex and diverse, specialist staff may be employed to seek and present the information to top management. In smaller companies it is usually a part of the responsibility of general management to do this work. The strengths and limitations of small companies may be all too apparent to their managers, but external issues require investigation in just the same way as they do by larger companies.

### The corporate audit
This should be a systematic investigation of all activities in the company. Each department in turn should be reviewed, and a clear description made of it in terms of:

– Type of operations carried out
– Number of personnel employed
– Skills and attitudes of personnel
– Nature of management structure and control
– Efficiency of tasks
– Relationships with other departments
– Relationships outside the company etc.

All departments can be analysed in this way. For example, in the marketing section of a company, under 'type of operations', a note might be made of activities such as market research, product promotions planning, advertising and aftersales service. Sufficient quantitative detail needs to be provided to give an idea of the scale of different activities. Market research activity, for instance, could involve anything from the occasional analysis of second hand statistics to full-blown field research exercises.

By making an 'audit' in this way, a good picture can be built up of the company's capabilities. Particular strengths and weaknesses will be highlighted which may have a significant effect on the choice of new products and their eventual success or lack of success. Even in small companies where managers feel that they already have clear knowledge of all activities, unexpected but important information will often emerge. In large companies, top management may find as a result of a critical analysis that long-held beliefs are no longer true. Functions like research and development for example often acquire a reputation for certain expertise on the basis of past achievements. Not until a disinterested assessment is made is it realised that most members of the staff possessing the expertise have retired or moved to other jobs and that new skills now predominate.

For production and other managers the concept of a corporate audit may be viewed with some reservation. Surveys suggest[4] that these managers tend to see their problems within a relatively short time scale – the production manager often feels he is judged by his ability to meet target output this *week* or this *month*. The need for departments such as production to be involved in product planning decisions is often accepted only with reluctance. It is a common view in companies that the production system should readily adapt to whatever demands are made upon it by new products. While all departments need to be able to adjust to necessary changes, there is no reason why new products should not be designed to capitalise on the strengths of the existing production system, rather than to compound its weaknesses. So the analysis of the production function should identify:

- The manufacturing processes where greatest expertise lies.
- Those processes which are fully utilised and those which offer spare capacity.
- The aptitudes and flexibility of workforce and management.
- The capabilities and strengths of particular production functions such as production control, quality control, stock control, etc.

- The nature of current products, the degree of standardisation of components and quantities manufactured.
- The scope and competence of production and industrial engineering functions.

The audit of the design department should follow the lines outlined in chapter 1. The exercise should be concerned more with facts rather than speculations about what could be achieved or why certain events had occurred in the past. This is particularly important when analysing departments such as design or research and development where historical events, determined by politically biased or unsound judgements, may give a false impression of true potential. All this information is needed before sound decisions can be made about new products. The information will also help managers to understand better the nature of their own departments and the way they relate to other functions in the company.

Once the audit has been completed and its findings accepted as accurate, it is necessary to ensure that the information remains up to date. Circumstances change in firms, sometimes very quickly, and frequent revisions may be necessary. Even after a design programme has been initiated, regular progress reviews should be made in the light of the latest information available (including that about the firm itself) and decisions taken whether to continue to the next review point or not.

**Analysis of external factors**
Companies need to investigate the environment in which they operate in order to identify competitive threats to existing products and market opportunities for new products. As in the case of the internal review of the firm which has just been considered, the extent of involvement of various managers in the external analysis will depend on the nature and structure of the firm. However, it is important that all managers have at least an understanding of the way threats and opportunities can be identified. This enables them to make a more informed contribution to new product decisions. What follows is an introduction to some means of investigating current market conditions and making predictions about future trends. This latter aspect is important because product design programmes, once initiated, may not generate new products for several months or even years, by which time the nature of the market might be quite different. In analysing the current market situation, information can be derived from

two sources – from within the company and from outside.

## Sources of information within the company

**Quantitative sources.** With increasingly widespread use of computers there can be large amounts of valuable information readily available in companies. In any case, in most firms the following data should be fairly easily obtainable:

- *Sales Figures.* These can indicate areas of growth or decline but may tell little about *overall* trends in the market unless the results of other companies are known as well. Sales figures can highlight the relative success of the firm's different products.
- *Financial data.* This should enable product areas of greatest profitability to be identified.
- *Purchasing trends.* Records may be available on recent trends and aspects of suppliers' quotations – for example delivery dates, the length of which may be a good indication of demand and activity.
- *Marketing data.* Depending on the type of company and the nature of its products, this may be a source of information about such things as advertising response rates, effects of promotional offers, results of recent market analyses.

**Qualitative sources.** There are many possibilities here; the problem is usually that of deciding which sources to tap and what mechanism to use to actually gather the information. Typical sources of qualitative information include:

- *Sales force reports.* Some companies require representatives to provide periodic commentaries on events in their areas. In this way, current information may be available on customers' actions and comments, competitors' activities (eg. test-marketing of new products, changes in prices) and general business trends (eg. news of short-time working, opening of new factories).
- *Other sources of 'informed opinion'.* Employees at all levels may have valuable information. Senior managers who are involved with outside activities may make contacts at high level during participation in meetings of professional bodies, employers' associations or at conferences. Less senior employees, whose work involves an awareness of current activities outside the company (for example, research scientists and personnel officers) should be encouraged to contribute as well.

- *Divisional and departmental reports.* Especially in large multi-centre companies, reports produced in one division may be of great value to other sections. Very large companies have full library and abstracting services to assist this flow of information.

## Sources of information outside the company.
**Statistical sources.** A large quantity of published statistical data is available to assist managers in understanding their business environments. Highly important in Britain are United Kingdom Governments statistics which are available in many forms covering a vast range of topics. They are generally considered to be reliable and most can be purchased easily by companies or examined in libraries. The Central Statistical Office provides several excellent guides[5,6,7] to help non-specialist managers use Government statistics to maximum advantage. Some of the best known statistical publications are:

- *Business Monitor Statistics*: United Kingdom sales figures on more than 5,000 product lines, published every three months.
- *Family Expenditure Survey*: Regional breakdown of household expenditure, published annually.
- *Census of Production*: Information about total purchases, sales, stocks, work in progress and other aspects of industrial production. Published annually in separate parts for each industry.

As well as Government statistics, there are statistics published by bodies such as:

- The National Economic Development Office.
- Trade associations (but frequently only available to member companies).
- Productivity councils and similar bodies.
- Commercial market research bureaux which often sell generalised data derived from market investigations commissioned by clients.

Although all these sources of statistical data can be extremely helpful to managers, it must be remembered that they all provide only 'secondary data'. In other words, information which has not been collected specifically for their particular needs. Consequently, it may require some 'interpretation' or 'adjustment', in which case managers need to understand the assumptions which they may be making. When satisfactory data cannot be obtained from published sources, 'primary' or 'field' research may be considered. This involves direct investigations perhaps utilising question-naires or interviews; it can be very expensive and is often not feasible for small companies.

**Qualitative sources.** Important indicators of present conditions and trends may be seen by regular inspection of items such as:

- *Trade journals*, particularly those relating to relevant areas of business.
- *Annual Reports* of companies which are engaged in similar types of operations to those of the manager's own firm;
- *Newspapers*, for example, the Financial Times and others with strong industrial and commercial sections;
- *T.V. and Radio programmes* which give a serious coverage of business and technological issues;
- *Conferences and exhibitions* where new ideas and techniques may be presented thus giving an idea of relative progress between firms.

On their own, none of these information sources can tell managers enough about market trends and opportunities to enable new product strategies to be developed. However they can provide valuable background information which may be coupled with the more rigorous data from other sources. This will allow managers in even small firms to build a comprehensive picture of their business environment and reduce the chances of missing opport-unities.

## 2.6 Second Planning Stage: Determining a Strategy for New Products

At this point, a number of areas may be seen where strengths within the company coincide with apparent opportunities in markets and the de-velopment of new products seems desirable. In other cases, for example where there are weaknesses in the company in functions like product design or production, it may be concluded that the best course is the acquisition of another company to obtain new products, or a merger with another firm or perhaps a re-direction of the firm's activities, say, from manufacturing into distribution of products made elsewhere. Where the decision *is* to develop new products, a strategy for doing this must be decided upon. In

determining this strategy the basic considerations are what skills and
resources the company has available (or can easily obtain), and which
market opportunities will be exploited. Then four steps of refinement are
needed:
- Forecasting future trends.
- Confirming areas of product interest.
- Calculating resources available for product development.
- Underwriting commitments to existing projects.

Each of these will now be considered.

### Step one: forecasting future trends

This needs to be done in respect of both the market and the products. For
the market, this means taking the information obtained about present and
historical conditions and making estimates about conditions in the future at
the time when the results of product development in the firm will be ready
for exploitation. Fundamental questions are:
- What will be the size of the total market?
- What will be the share of the market held by competitors?
- What share of the market can we expect to gain?

Simply projecting sales figures into the future and analysing individual
company performance can give rise to falsely optimistic expectations. Just
because total annual sales of a certain type of product have risen steadily for
the last four years, say, there may be no guarantee that they will continue to
do so for the next four years. Customers' tastes, actions by home and
foreign competition, social and political trends, and availability of credit
are just a few of the factors that may have to be considered. The longer the
anticipated product development period, the more uncertainty there will
be. For further discussion on the complexities of market forecasting,
reference should be made to specialist publications.[8,9,10]

As far as products are concerned, predictions also need to be made. What
will be the nature of products in the future? What level of performance will
be the norm? What size? What fuel consumption? What speed of
operation?

Information about technical aspects may be revealed by the use of
various techniques of *Technological Forecasting* (TF). Again appropriate
references[11,12] should be consulted for a full discussion of the many

different approaches which can be used. The two techniques which are outlined here have been included because they are relatively reliable and easy to use.

**Trend extrapolation.** In the same way that historical market data (eg. sales figures) can be plotted and projected to give future estimates, then so can data on measurable technical features of products. As an example, consider the results that might be obtained if the feature 'speed of operation' for electric kettles was examined; data as shown in *figure 2.5* might be obtained.

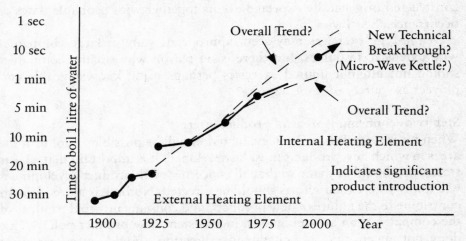

*Figure 2.5  Speed of Operation of Electric Kettles*

It will be noticed that for each technical system, refinement occurs until the boiling speed reaches a level where little further improvement is obtainable, and the plot flattens. Not until a new technical system is achieved (in this case the placing of the element inside the kettle instead of strapping it below the base) does improvement continue until a further plateau is reached. This feature of technical progress is sometimes referred to as the *S-curve phenomenon* because of the shape of the plots obtained. The problem for forecasters is to decide the nature of the overall trend. In this case, has the ultimate level of performance been achieved – or is a major technical breakthrough about to occur? If so, what will be the effect on product design plans? Wills[11] gives further examples concerning features of computers, hovercraft and aircraft.

**Delphi Forecasting Method.** This is a method of assembling the expert opinion which is necessary to interpret the sort of quantitative data that is involved in extrapolating trends – for example, in the case just examined, to decide which of the alternatives is the overall trend or the one most likely to occur. Typically, a Delphi exercise is carried out by asking experts (in the areas being explored) to consider a list of possible future events and to say when, if ever, they expect each to occur, with explanations. The answers are correlated and extreme replies investigated. Eventually a scenario is constructed of generally expected events together with probable dates of occurrence. (See Twiss.[12])

Delphi-type exercises may seem appropriate only in large companies with extensive resources, but there is no reason why smaller companies should not attempt limited exercises perhaps using knowledgeable employees as sources of information.

### Step two: confirming areas of product interest

When future trends have been evaluated, it will be possible to confirm the areas in which new products must be developed. It is important that a clear statement should be made so that all concerned with product development will know where their efforts should be directed. Nothing is more likely to contribute to the failure of new products, and consequently to the failure of the company, than an ambiguous, inconsistent new product policy. This does not mean that no change of direction should ever occur; as circumstances alter, firms must be ready to curtail some design projects and to start new ones. But such action must be based on sound information and not the intuition or faint-heartedness of managers.

### Step three: calculating resources available for product development

Developing new products can be highly expensive. The company needs to decide how much it can afford to allocate to new products, bearing in mind that a continuing commitment will be required. Individual projects may last for several years and there is little point in starting unless funds will be available for the whole period.

In calculating funds the company must look at the financial reserves it has available including its ability to raise loans from banks and cash from shareholders. It must also predict future levels of costs, sales and profits. Projects must then be devised which are well within the financial scope available, always remembering that some new products are eventually unsuccessful. In framing its commitment to development work, it is desirable that the firm should allocate a fixed percentage of annual turnover. This is better than relating allocations to profit since in many companies this will mean some years with adequate funds interspersed by others where little or no cash is available. A low level of steady support is better than widely fluctuating support even if this involves a higher average level.

Not all the resources needed for product development are financial. Adequate managerial competence must be available together with specific skills and experience. Workshops and test equipment may be needed, together with the co-operation of various departments; for example, the production department in providing access to normal manufacturing equipment for test purposes.

### Step four: underwriting commitments to existing projects

Amidst enthusiasm for a new product programme it is vital that any existing projects are not forgotten. Before a final decision is taken to allocate time and money to the programme, the continuing needs of any new products already under development must be assessed. It is particularly important to reinforce the morale of those working on existing projects by a restatement of commitment to them. The enthusiasm of senior managers for new ventures may cause unease and uncertainty amongst staff unless consistent support is given to their projects as well. Sometimes managers allow their fascination with latest ideas to undermine their responsibilities for other projects which are still important, but happen to have reached a mundane stage in development such as that concerned with repetitive testing and improvement.

## 2.7 Third Planning Stage: Screening and Selection of Specific New Product Ideas

So far new product decisions will have been considered in the general sense of product types and market areas. Now it is time to decide about the adoption of specific ideas for new products. First, companies need to investigate the sources of ideas available to them, then to evaluate ideas in a way that will enable them to choose those with the greatest potential.

**Sources of ideas for new products.**
Within most companies there will be individuals with a talent for producing ideas for new products. Such people are likely to be working in research or design departments where they will be encouraged to explain and develop their ideas. However, creativity is not necessarily confined to these areas of a company and many useful ideas can be obtained from production, marketing, or other departments if the opportunity exists for information to flow. Some companies use suggestion schemes for this purpose or make a point of having 'open door' policies so that product ideas (and other topics) can be freely discussed with managers. In addition some firms arrange seminars or conferences so that employees (particularly sales representatives and supervisory staff) can meet and discuss points of interest including means by which present products and services can be improved or new ones developed.

The problem with ideas generated internally, however, is that they tend to reflect company needs rather than customer needs. For this reason, ideas originating outside the company may have greater promise. Customers' ideas and needs, if they can be defined directly, are more likely to lead to commercially attractive products. Market research techniques may be used to identify the needs of both consumer and industrial markets,[13] although in some industries it is common for customers to make direct requests for new products (e.g. defence equipment) which, when developed, join the company's range of standard products.

Sometimes private inventors or other companies may offer to sell ideas or proposals which they are unable to develop themselves. These may be useful and worth considering, but it is important to consider the reasons why the invention is being sold. Are there serious weaknesses in the idea? Is expensive development required? Also, unpleasant misunderstandings may arise if such proposals are not handled carefully. If a proposal is declined because the company is already working on similar lines, the eventual launching of the product may bring accusations of plagiarism from the inventor. As a general rule, managers should insist that an outside inventor always files an application for a patent before disclosing his idea.

Companies may actively seek out such ideas by advertising for them, or by having 'new products competitions' or by sponsoring research in universities, research establishments, etc. Some companies subscribe to research associations which give members the option of taking over promising lines of research. Large companies may have a 'scanning department' whose job it is to check publications for news of ideas. Journals, reports, newspapers etc. should be monitored as well as specialist publications such as the bulletins of inventions which are published by the National Research Development Corporation (now a part of the British Technology Group), a body which helps to bring together inventors and companies.

### Screening and selection of ideas for new products

It is easy to be either unduly euphoric or pessimistic about individual ideas. To avoid this, a screening or evaluation procedure should be devised which examines each proposal against a set of basic criteria. For most companies a two stage procedure is sufficient; a quick screening to eliminate the weakest ideas, followed by a more thorough investigation of the survivors.

The quick screening should be conducted using a checklist of essential parameters; failure at any point means rejection of the idea. The nature of the parameters will depend on a company's individual requirements and should be set by top management – an important aspect of design policy. However, the screening against these parameters can then be carried out by less senior personnel. Examples of the factors which could be specified include:

- Market characteristics (e.g. at least 15% market share attainable, growth rate of 5% p.a. required).
- Profit on investment (e.g. 25% gross annually).
- Production facilities (e.g. must not require new equipment to produce)
- Competitive advantages
- Service facilities, etc.

Skinner[8] gives a specimen checklist with ten factors.

This initial screening may eliminate up to 90% of the original ideas. The remainder should then be analysed in detail starting with those ideas which the initial screening indicated as being most attractive. Basically, the detailed evaluation will cover the same grounds as the quick screening but in much greater depth. This is necessary to identify as far as possible the extent of the risks involved in the proposed new project and to confirm that the company is able to carry these risks. In general the evaluation should examine:

- *Product characteristics*. A full definition of the idea with details of size, features, selling price, etc. This is essential to allow accurate estimates of effects of competition, costs involved, manufacturing problems etc.
- *Marketing aspects*. i.e. customers' requirements, competitors' activities, segmentation, distribution etc.
- *Manufacturing aspects*. i.e. plant requirements, storage, handling, skills etc.
- *Financial aspects*. i.e. cost of the design programme, sales needed to recover overheads etc.
- *Social, political and legal aspects*. Considerations here might be those of pollution (caused by the new product itself or during its manufacture), or possibly problems associated with the supply of raw materials from a politically unstable country. From the legal point of view there may be features of new product proposals which require attention such as patent infringement or statutory regulations concerning design features.

Many publications are available to help managers carry out effective evaluation. Particularly useful are two checklists published by the British Institute of Management.[14] Detailed information about product planning can be found in the books by Skinner[8], Holt[15] and White.[16] A highly readable account of the experiences of several companies during their attempts to choose and design new products is provided by Blakstad[17]; Carson and Rickards[18] give a detailed presentation of a method for identifying new product ideas.

## Design Brief
The result of these planning activities should be a firm proposal for a design project. If the work has been done competently, the prospects for success should be good. Assuming that the internal and external analyses have been accurate, the selection of product parameters appropriate and the evaluation of ideas against them consistent, then the final outcome will depend upon the skill and efficiency applied to the actual design stage which follows. In order to ensure the best design results, a design brief should be prepared. The purpose of this document (which is discussed in detail in later

chapters) is to give guidance about the resources available for the design work and to confirm the specification which the new product must satisfy.

## 2.8 Conclusion

This chapter has been concerned with the issues that must be considered by managers before any design work can begin. For many companies the important first step is to become aware of the vulnerability of existing products and the nature of the threats which may be directed to them. The problem of avoiding design gaps has been discussed and the need for a coherent product strategy was stressed.

Strong support was given to the view that designers, particularly specialists from outside the company, should be involved in this work, even though this is not their traditional role. The grounds for this view exist because designers can bring a wide knowledge of current trends into the decision making process and because their training and methods of tackling problems enable them to see opportunities that might not be apparent to managers or technical specialists. This does not mean that designers should be given sole responsibility for this work; there is plenty of evidence to indicate that the most successful companies are those where designers and others work together in multi-disciplinary teams where communications are good and problems are tackled collaboratively.

# 3 Case Study: Beta Engineering

## 3.1 Introduction

This case study reports actual events. However all of the names have been changed. Beta Engineering has factories in several parts of the United Kingdom and employs about 14,000 people. Its business could be described as 'general manufacturing' since it produces a range of products and sub-assemblies mainly for industrial customers. Functionally, it is organised into several sections, each of which produces a family of products. These sections operate independently of each other with separated functions such as production, marketing, sales etc. Until recently this organisation seemed to work well. Each section has enjoyed a steady level of activity, generally supplying long runs of products to a small number of industrial customers. As a consequence, the company has tended to develop very strong manufacturing skills and organisation, but has weak marketing and sales operations.

A few years ago, senior managers in the company recognised that dependence on a few customers and product lines could be dangerous. The need was seen for diversification into new areas and also for a general infusion of new products. Product design work was already carried out in each section, but it was limited in scope and was mainly concerned with modifications to existing product designs.

The Board decided to set up a central *Product Design Department* (PDD) which would develop product ideas to the point where they would be handed over to one of the manufacturing sections. It was thought that this department would stand a better chance of yielding viable new products than would expanded design groups within the individual sections. It was argued that these were so strongly production-oriented that creativity and innovation were effectively suppressed. Furthermore, it was recognised that ideas for new products were needed from outside the traditional areas of business. Again, preoccupation with manufacturing aspects meant that existing sections were ill-equipped to undertake the generation and subsequent evaluation of ideas.

Thus PDD was set up in a self-contained building on one of the company's sites in the south of England. Its chief, Mr Page, was appointed to the Board as director with special responsibility for design and new products. So in theory, as *figure 3.1* shows, PPD was an operating unit of similar status to each of the manufacturing sections which were also represented by their respective directors on the Board. Mr Page was given a free hand to organise and run PPD. His brief was simply 'to design and develop new products'. He responded by building up a group of engineers and designers, and also established a well equipped workshop.

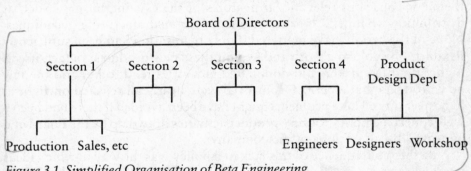

*Figure 3.1 Simplified Organisation of Beta Engineering*

Within a short time he had identified several promising ideas for new products and work proceeded on their development. However, after several years of work on these and further ideas, considerable sums of money had been spent, but no commercially successful products had evolved; the department was closed amidst disillusionment and anxiety. Looking back over the operation of PPD a number of valuable lessons emerge for other companies contemplating setting up this kind of new product unit.

## 3.2 Need for a Design Policy

After reaching its decision that there was a need to move away from familiar product areas, the top management of Beta failed to analyse the existing business to see what type of new products would seem logical. Instead of seeking to build on existing strengths in the company, it was left to Mr Page to decide what avenues to pursue. His suggestions were usually supported to start with, but after a period of expenditure on design work it was often the case that the Board would begin to question the relevance of the work. Usually this led to a reduction of resources and effort on that particular line of development until it was finally scrapped.

This lack of guidelines for new product work made life difficult for Mr Page. On the one hand he had the advantage of freedom of approach to his work, on the other hand he had the disadvantage of an unlimited choice of areas in which to try to find new opportunities. This gave rise to a bewildering mixture of different design projects without any common theme or conscious relevance to features of the existing business such as distribution channels, market segments, or manufacturing techniques. None of this would have mattered if the organisation had been sufficiently flexible to be able to absorb and exploit these new products. In fact, it was highly rigid (as production-dominated industries tend to be) and the few new products that emerged from PDD were nearly all rejected outright at handover time. These problems might have been avoided if there had been a well-conceived policy for new product activities drawn up by the Board and approved by all sections of the company.

A further consequence of this lack of a policy was the way in which ideas for new products were sought and evaluated. If a limited field of investigation had been defined, many sources of ideas could have been analysed with thoroughness. With an unlimited field so many ideas were available that few received, at best, more than just cursory examination. The main criterion for the further examination of an idea tended to be the inherent interest it had to Mr Page, rather than a more rational alignment against a previously formulated guideline.

## 3.3 Need for a Balanced Approach to New Product Work

The Product Design Department had a staff of engineering designers, and workshop technicians. At no time did it see the need to recruit any industrial designers or marketing or financial personnel. As a result of this technical bias it was not surprising to find that new product ideas were assessed mainly in terms of engineering feasibility – the only non-technical assessment being carried out by Mr Page, himself an engineering specialist. In this respect, the organisation of PDD reflected the rest of Beta which, as already noted, was strong technically but weak in marketing skills. The fact that ideas were selected for development mainly on their technical potential inevitably led to a high percentage of product failures. The markets which it had been assumed 'must exist for technically superior products' were usually found *not* to be there when the new idea was presented to the world.

Another result of this imbalance between engineering and marketing skills was that even when ideas with real all-round potential were selected, the wrong kinds of features were built into the products. So, for example, PDD found that one new product, which boasted a very compact design but was rather noisy in operation, did not sell very well. Eventually, it was realised that customers did not care about the size of the product, but did demand silent operation. Months of work to perfect an ingenious design were unnecessarily wasted. Reference at the project planning stage to a consultant designer experienced in the field and the preparation of a proper product specification would have avoided the problem.

The lesson here is that companies must find out what the customer really wants and then design the product to suit. Most readers will say that there is nothing new about this statement (which is true), but the fact remains that many companies *do* spend money on the development of products that no one wants. Particularly in traditional companies producing industrial goods, there is a mistrust of 'marketing' where the misconception persists that the subject is exclusively about pressure selling, advertising and complicated mathematical modelling beyond the comprehension of ordinary managers. This is a pity since a few elementary techniques of market research could greatly assist many companies to improve their product success rates.

## 3.4 Need for Consistent Top Management Support

The Board set up PDD with the expectation that it would quickly generate new products. As months, and then years, passed without the successful completion of many of the design projects, the directors began to question whether money was being spent wisely. Because product ideas were only briefly evaluated when selected for development, there was plenty of scope for subsequent doubts. If the company went through a bad financial patch, funds were hastily withdrawn from PDD. At other times, when cash was easier, Mr Page was urged to 'speed up' the work on his most promising projects so that favourable reports could be given to shareholders and customers. Invariably, as these things happen, when Mr Page needed money for some important line of work, cash was tight and he had to modify his plans. The effect of this 'stop-go' policy was to damage seriously the efficiency of the design work. To the people working in PDD it seemed that in one month top managers were desperate for results, in the next month they wished the department didn't exist. The engineers and designers became frustrated and insecure, which in turn affected the quality of their work.

Once again, the problem could be traced back to the setting up of PDD. As well as failing to ask 'what do we expect to achieve?', the Board also failed to ask 'what expenditure can we consistently afford, over what period?' All companies need to provide solid top management support for new product ventures backed by consistent allocations of funds. However, this can be done with confidence only if the total design costs have been estimated with a fair degree of accuracy before a project is approved. These costs will depend upon the scale of the project, the degree to which the technology is unfamiliar and the range of solutions that will be needed to impress the market. In most cases, none of this information was available when decisions were made in PDD.

## 3.5 Need for Inter-Functional Participation

PDD was designed to be independent of the other sections of the company in its day–to–day activities.It had been envisaged that as the design of each product was completed it would be handed over to one of the manufacturing sections and then work would start on the next project. By being able to concentrate on design without getting side-tracked into routine problems in production or elsewhere, it was expected that a specialist PDD would be more successful than if it was attached to one or more of the sections. In fact, the managers of the manufacturing sections resented being presented with new products by what they saw as an outside unit. Although they saw a need for new business, it hurt their pride to have ideas forced upon them – a classic example of the frequently cited 'Not Invented Here' syndrome.

Perhaps the mistake lay in the concept of isolating PDD. Whilst it is true that design work may need some protection from the crises and distractions of day–to–day operations, this does not rule out the need for co-operation. In many cases managers may have had good reasons for resisting new products – perhaps they did not have the right machinery, capacity or skills available. But with real interaction from the start of each development project between the manufacturing sections and PDD (and customers, too) there would have been a much better chance of new products emerging that had general acceptability.

## 3.6 Conclusion

The basic reason behind the failure of the Product Design Department was an absence of 'total' design management. Contact with the company during the several years that the department was in operation clearly showed that the project failures were not brought about by a shortage of practical design skills. It is true that the balance of these skills was weighed too much in favour of engineering aspects at the expense of styling and other requirements but this was not the fundamental problem besetting the department. (One new product received a national design award and several others attracted favourable comment – none of which helped to make commercial impact, unfortunately.)

The real problem was that the task of formulating a strategy for new products had not been taken in hand and the researching and planning of individual projects was carried out inadequately as well. The real failure was at the top management level – not so much the director of PDD, who was a highly competent designer and a good motivator of staff – but the Board of the company which had failed to develop an appropriate design policy and give him the necessary support. None of the aspects of design policy discussed in chapter 1 had received anything like adequate attention.

The setting of design objectives, for example, had been done with little reference to the long-term results that were desired. Indeed, what was wanted had hardly been thought through at all – there was just a feeling that something needed to be done to reduce dependence on existing products.

As a result, the design objectives were stated in very broad terms and were not drawn up formally existing only as an 'understanding' between the Board members. Defining and setting design standards was left to the director of the design department who attended to this on a purely personal basis rather than preparing any guidelines for his staff to work against. Audits of design activity and evaluation of design results were undertaken by the Board but, as the last few pages describe, only in an erratic manner, usually when some crisis was occurring. Even the structure and organisation of the design activity was left to the department to sort out for itself.

Hence the overall result was an aimless and under-achieving design department caused by a top management which failed to understand its responsibilities for deciding design policy. The consequences of their decision to opt out of these responsibilities by giving the director of the design department a 'free hand' stands as a warning to other companies.

# 4 Organising Design Activities

## 4.1 Introduction

The discussion of the Beta Engineering case in the preceding chapter was intended to highlight the factors which may influence the outcome of design projects. Prominent amongst those factors was the question of organising for design activities. Senior management must consider very carefully the special features of design work and design departments; it is then necessary to decide how best to structure such departments and how they may work with and relate to other parts of the company.

Several different structures may be encountered in practice and some of these are discussed in this chapter. Some companies organise themselves in the Beta fashion with separate design units headed by a senior manager to whom is delegated (or abandoned) part or all of the responsibility for product design and strategy decisions. At the extreme are companies whose design activities are diffused throughout the organisation. In this case, top management may or may not set policy guidelines or seek to ensure some degree of conformity in design results.

Some companies identify a role for 'product champions' to push new product projects through any organisational or procedural barriers which may be encountered. In such companies, a 'task force' approach is quite common with small groups of engineers, designers and others assigned to specific projects. Other companies may prefer to use a more broadly based method, perhaps built on one or more large units within which there are a number of projects. Individuals move in or out of these projects depending upon the need for their particular skills. It is clear from the available literature that there is little agreement about the precise circumstances in which each method should be applied, although it is possible to derive guidance in broad terms about selecting a suitable approach.

Whatever organisational structure is adopted, leadership and management will be required. Some experts see a need for a special kind of 'design manager' who, amongst other functions, is able to bridge the knowledge and language gap that frequently exists between ordinary managers and designers.[1,2]

Hence, the purpose of this chapter is to examine these organisational questions and to try to give an idea of the advantages and disadvantages of the alternative structures that may be adopted. The special demands placed upon those who manage design are compared with the demands placed upon managers in other functions. Following from this, it is possible to draw some conclusions about the personal characteristics that should be sought in those who manage design activities.

## 4.2 Concepts of Change

All managers are confronted by change – if no change ever occurred then there would be no need to have managers at all. If markets were static or totally predictable, no-one would need to take decisions about production quotas. If customers' tastes and loyalties never changed then no new products would be needed. But, of course, in the real world change is an ever-present fact of life. For millions of different reasons – some natural, some man-made, some accidental, some deliberate – all companies must continually adjust their activities to compensate for changes which are taking place. In the same way that changes in the market dictate a need for product design, the act of designing new products, or improving old ones, gives rise to some degree of change within the company. This change may be slight, as when modifications are made to minor components, or it may be major, as in the case where a factory must be totally re-organised and re-equipped to accommodate a new product.

Regardless of its extent however, many organisations will resist change right up to the point where survival of the organisation is seen to be at stake. In the normal course of events, preoccupation with current activities may leave little scope for any real innovation. Many firms demonstrate this attitude by paying lip-service to their product design activities whilst proclaiming official doctrines of innovation. Such firms may, for example, encourage new product ideas, only to find consistently that none of them meets the stringent criteria laid down in advance.[3] Similarly, many firms effectively eliminate change by oscillating between support and resistence – an 'on-again, off-again' approach to design and innovation.

Not infrequently, a myopic concentration on the manufacture of existing products means that new products are never successfully developed. Greiner[4] is critical of this attitude to new methods and products. He reinforces the opinion that successful change does not begin until strong environmental and internal pressures 'shake the power structure at its very foundation'. A more recent publication[5], appearing in the depths of the worst economic recession for 50 years, still finds it necessary to challenge managers to consider the implications of failures to adjust to change and urges them to be receptive to innovation.

According to Twiss[6], resistance to change is more often a feature of older companies than younger ones. He has found that as companies reach maturity, strategies become more defensive and fewer projects lead to new products which depart substantially from current practice. He believes that the reason for this often lies with the 'Chief Technologist' who is normally found to be the creative force in a young company but is less effective as the company evolves and a management team is built up around him. This means that in the mature company it becomes necessary to design some formal approach in order to cope with change.

An American study by Lynton[7] has examined large and small organis-ations and found that each may face circumstances in which they can no longer deal with change by intuitive means. It may be thought that an organisation's size is the primary factor in handling change. But Lynton has found that a decision to formally cope with change is not so much related to the size of the organisation, as to the degrees of uncertainty in technology, markets and the environment. The necessary redesign of the organisation into one which can accommodate higher degrees of uncertainty is invariably more difficult in older companies but is not markedly so in larger companies as opposed to smaller ones. New designs always involve some change and for this reason they may be resisted. After all, whilst the modern company is often built around the production process which is (usually) rational and standardised, design is not always seen as rational and can be disruptive to those affected by it. Bright[8] offers 12 reasons (*table 4.1.*) why an innovative change such as a new design may be resisted by the employees of a company.

1   To protect social status.
2   To protect an existing way of life.
3   To prevent devaluation of capital invested in an existing facility.
4   To prevent a reduction of livelihood because the change would devalue the knowledge or skills presently required.
5   To prevent the elimination of a job or profession.
6   To avoid expenditure such as the cost of replacing existing equipment.
7   Because the change opposes social customs, fashions and tastes and the habits of everyday life.
8   Because the change conflicts with existing laws.
9   Because of rigidity inherent in large or bureaucratic organisations.
10  Because of personality, habit, fear, equilibrium between individuals or institutions, status and similar social and psychological considerations.
11  Because of tendency of organised groups to force conformity.
12  Because of the reluctance of an individual or group to disturb the equilibrium of society or the business atmosphere.

*Table 4.1 Reasons for Resisting an Innovative Change.*

It is interesting that the book in which the list first appeared was published some 20 years ago – and it is 60 years since the pioneering work of Elton Mayo and others[9] drew attention to the importance of developing good human relations within companies. Yet still the lessons do not seem to be generally understood. It is true that there are companies apparently able to adjust to change with the support and commitment of the whole workforce. But there seem to be many others which are quite unable to cope because their employees, including managers, fear change and consequently block the progress which is necessary for survival. It would be misleading to generalise about underlying causes, but since management is given (or assumes) responsibility for managing, this is where the basic problem must be sought. Managers who cannot tolerate uncertainty and seek to avoid change, or who are unable to communicate with their subordinates or see no need to do so, are not suited to the task of managing product design or similar change-inducing activities.

Not only is change itself important, so is the rate of change in a company. A firm has to change at a sufficient rate and in an ordered manner to meet the conditions imposed from outside. A rate which is too high leads to chaos; one which is too low may end in bankruptcy. Also, in order to achieve the goal of prosperity which is the reason for the existence of most companies, the effects of competition demand that each subsequent design change has to be done a little better and a little more profitably than the preceding one. It is disturbing that so few organisations seem prepared for this challenge. Many are engulfed in systems which perpetuate conformity, precedent and procedure, and reaction to crisis, continues to be the primary model of adjusting to change.

The problem is huge (and in its entirety is quite outside the scope of this discussion) involving issues of governmental policies, the attitudes and activities of trade unions, divisions of wealth and power and the availability of resources such as fuel and materials. However, as already noted, one major factor is the style of management which is practised and encouraged in design and other innovative activities. Efficiency in recognising the need for new products and the careful screening and selecting of ideas will all be in vain if the management of the company is not suited to the special requirements of new product work. The nature of these requirements can be better understood if the special features of design departments are compared with those of other departments, particularly production with which design is often closely linked, since both are often considered to be the 'technical' parts of the business and to have similar methods of

| Features of Production | Features of Design |
|---|---|
| 1 Rational, standardised, predictable | 1 Irrational, novel, unpredictable |
| 2 Operations accurately timed | 2 Accurate timing of activities usually impossible |
| 3 Long runs of identical products | 3 Activities frequently changing |
| 4 Creativity and initiative not developed in workforce | 4 Highly creative personnel essential |
| 5 Work closely controlled – essential for profitability. Risk eliminated | 5 Profitability related to skill, change, judgment, intuition, risk taking, etc. |

*Table 4.2 Comparison of Organisational Features of Production with those of Product Design*

operation. *Table* 4.2 summarises the main organisational features which distinguish design and production.

Comparison with other functions such as marketing or finance will also show differences of emphasis; for example, marketing's need for short lead times on new products compared with design's concern to spend as long as possible on projects to achieve the best results. In the light of these differences, we need to consider both the organisation of the design unit itself, and its relationship with the rest of the company.

## 4.3 Organisation of Product Design Units

A number of years ago Burns and Stalker[10] analysed the organisational aspects of a sample of firms involved with the design of new products; their work remains important today. They observed that within these companies there were organisational styles ranging from what they termed 'mechanistic' which were very formal, hierarchial, bureaucratic and inflexible, to styles which they termed 'organic' which were informal, based on teams and tended to 'shape' themselves to the problems being tackled.

They concluded that mechanistic systems work satisfactorily only where conditions are relatively stable – flow line production departments for example, or other situations where close control of highly specialised work is essential. Mechanistic forms of organisation are not likely to prove satisfactory when applied to design units, which need flexibility in many respects. Here organic systems are more appropriate and, as Burns and Stalker observed, such systems improve the prospects of success for new products. *Table* 4.3 lists some of the features that may be found in organic systems. Managers responsible for product design departments need to consider how they can promote 'organic features'.

1   Unifying theme is the 'common task' – each individual contributes special knowledge and skills – individual's tasks are constantly re-defined as the total situation changes.
2   Hierarchy does not predominate – problems are not referred up or down, but are tackled on a team basis.
3   Flexibility – jobs not precisely defined.

4 Control is through the 'common goal' rather than by institutions, rules and regulations.

5 Expertise and knowledge located throughout the organisation not just at the top.

6 Communications consist of information and advice rather than instructions and decisions.

*Table 4.3 Typical Features of Organic Systems*

Promoting such features may be a delicate matter, especially within those firms which are otherwise organised along precise and inflexible lines. Even in situations where they do not have the opportunity to develop ideal systems, managers should be aware of the actions they can take to assist creative work so that organisationally desirable features predominate. Whitfield[11], discussing a range of issues associated with creativity and innovation, shows that design teams are likely to be most effective where:

– All members make a full contribution; co-operation is accepted as the way of achieving the best result.

– Short term leadership tends to rotate according to the immediate needs of the job.

– Decisions are made by the people who are best informed on the subject. These are not necessarily the most senior present.

It is important to understand that mechanistic and organic styles are categories of organisation which are unlikely, in practice, to be found in 'pure' forms. There are many intermediate stages between these categories and most design units will exhibit features of both styles, with the 'right balance' depending on the nature of the company, the industry and the projects being undertaken. In all cases, the best policy for the design manager is to be vigilant for the evolving of mechanistic characteristics and then take steps to prevent them becoming dominant within the design operation. The kind of features that need to be checked include:

– Increase in the number of levels of supervision.

– Control by detailed inspection of work methods rather than by evaluation of results.

– Communication consisting of instructions and decisions rather than exchange of advice, consultation or information.

– Confrontation of win-lose nature rather than collaboration.

- Insular attitude of top management with sense of commitment to past decisions.

The role of the design manager is clearly a crucial one in promoting successful results. In many respects the qualities required in order to be effective in this job are substantially different from those traditionally exhibited by managers. The main emphasis must be on the design manager's ability to deal with change and ambiguity[12]; *table* 4.4 summarises the main differences.

| The Traditional Manager | The Design Manager |
|---|---|
| 1 Experience-based know-how. Education as one-time activity. | 1 Managerial knowledge based on recurrent up-dating. |
| 2 Technical and analytical skills emphasised. | 2 Skills needed to deal with ambiguity, complexity and conflict. |
| 3 Expectation of continuity of organisational experiences. | 3 Ability to adapt to unpredictable new events. |
| 4 Standard operating procedures guide decisions. | 4 Decisions augmented by environmental and other inputs. |
| 5 Inward perception emphasises internal, issues, competition. | 5 Inward/outward perception includes societal problems. |
| 6 Importance attached to stable relationships. | 6 Temporary relationships tolerated. |
| 7 Assumes rational organisational behaviour. | 7 Rationality seen as subjective. |
| 8 Task orientated. | 8 Goal orientated. |
| 9 Action oriented to keep physically busy. | 9 Combines periods of reflection with action. |
| 10 Individualistic approach to specialised problem solving. | 10 Interdisciplinary team approach to complex problem solving. |

*Table 4.4 Differences in Managerial Roles*

## 4.4 Location of Design within the Firm

It is not always easy to decide where design activities should be located within the firm. As already stated, product design is often considered to be a technical activity of a kind similar to production. However, because of the fundamentally different natures of the two functions, giving control of design to production may result in failure. This may happen either because organisational conditions inappropriate to design are imposed or simply because production has resistance to new products (because of the disruption involved). This resistance may take the form of constant rejections of new designs, refusal to supply information and help, or just general obstruction – all while paying lip-service to the need for new products. These attitudes may be particularly acute in long-established firms where design work has been limited previously to improvements and modifications. Nevertheless, in a great many companies design departments, are to be found as part of the production set-up, under the control of a production or technical manager, as in *figure 4.1.*

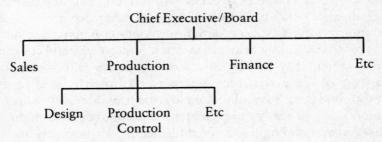

*Figure 4.1 Design as Part of Production*

It will be noted that design is effectively isolated from the highest level decision maker, the chief executive. Information and directives may be 'filtered' by production to the extent that design work is reduced to a mundane level. Modifications to existing designs and extensions to current ranges of products may well be achieved, but more ambitious projects are likely to be stifled. Any work that is undertaken will be subject to pressure to ensure that production considerations are given paramount attention – at the expense of other requirements including those of the customer.

Several of the case studies in this book highlight the limitations caused by treating design as a component of production. Very similar problems may arise if design is organised as a part of one of the other functions such as marketing.

Some companies seek to avoid these problems by establishing design as an independent department equal in status to the other major functions, as shown in *figure 4.2.*

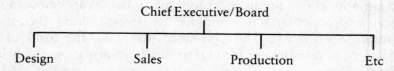

*Figure 4.2  Design as an Independent Function*

This may well lead to improved design performance because with direct linkage to the highest decision level, projects can be monitored and encouraged. Radical projects may be attempted and some success anticipated. However, some drawbacks will remain. The design manager (or design director) may have to bargain with other departmental bosses for cash and resources. Because design is a long-term activity it may seem to senior managers in other functions that it is just a wasteful consumer of the income which they create. Boardroom politics may work to the disadvantage of the design function; power is often related to the size of financial budgets. Sales directors or finance directors whose scale of operation may be many times greater than that of design, might acquire or assume correspondingly greater influence in decision-making. A further disadvantage with an independent design unit is that it may well be viewed with suspicion by the rest of the firm. The fact that it *is* separate from other functions may cause speculation about its relevance to company objectives. This usually manifests itself when a new product is ready to be handed over at the end of a design exercise. The product may be rejected because it is seen as an intrusion from outside – sometimes referred to as the 'not invented here' syndrome.

Some companies try to overcome this problem by directing new product operations through a steering committee which represents all major functions. Others appoint 'project champions' whose job it is to push the new product through all barriers and solve any problems which may arise.

Unfortunately, project champions are not often given the authority which is a necessary for them to be effective. Companies sometimes delude themselves into believing that a bright young manager will be able to achieve the progress that has been denied to others simply by force of personality. Frequently, the problem is not one of leadership at all, but of availability and allocation of resources. For example, if the design unit needs to use a particular manufacturing process for test purposes and that process is fully occupied with production work designated as top priority by the Board, then no amount of dynamic design management will ensure success.

Despite these reservations, the steering committee approach as summarised in *figure 4.3*, does offer a number of advantages. The most important is the potential ability of the committee to ensure both the relevance of new design activities and the acceptability of design results.

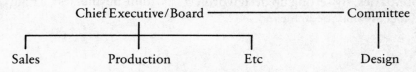

*Figure 4.3  Design Guided by Steering Committee*

The intimate involvement of the committee members, drawn from all major areas of the company, should promote well-integrated design, in theory at least. In practice, the method may be less successful. As well as the usual problems associated with management by committee – compromise, indecision and procrastination – individual managers may still succeed in undermining projects which they find undesirable. These managers may find that conflict arises out of their dual roles (as departmental managers and as steering committee members) and that this causes the taking of inappropriate decisions.[13] The use of a 'project champion' in place of a committee may avoid many of these problems, although selecting the right person for the job assumes crucial importance. Ideally, the champion needs to have all the qualities of the change-responsive manager listed in *table 4.4*. In addition, he must be able to understand the technical aspects of the project and do his best to deliver an acceptable new product within the deadlines set. Whilst satisfying colleagues elsewhere in the firm, he must always see the completion of the project as the main priority and he must

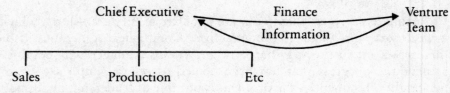

*Figure 4.4  The Venture Concept*

inspire his team towards this goal.

In order to encourage this approach, some firms move one step further still and, except for a 'financing link', effectively set free the design project so that it can grow and mature independently of the main organisation. This concept of organising for new products is sometimes referred to as the 'venture method'. It is especially attractive for traditionally organised companies which find it difficult to manage design within its normal boundaries. By setting up design projects as 'mini-businesses', a high degree of success may be achieved.


## 4.5 Organising for Design Outside the Company

Up to now, the discussion has been based upon the assumption that design work is being carried out within the company. Of course, this is not always the case; for a variety of reasons, design may have to take place outside the company. Projects may be handed over to a specialist outside design consultancy when suitable resources do not exist within the firm, or where they are already fully stretched by other projects. Typically, this may happen when a firm is attempting to move into a new product area of which it has little direct technical experience; rather than build up a new design group, it may decide to go outside, at least as far as the 'mark one' version of the product is concerned. Once the new concept has established itself in the market, it may then be appropriate to set up an internal design operation.

Other firms may use outside design consultancies as concept generators. In order to get around any creative blocks within the company the intitial design work may be done outside followed by a shortened development programme of testing and refinement inside the firm. Finally, a few companies make a practice of sub-contracting all of their design activities, usually in the expectation of achieving very high standards in design results coupled with short project durations. This approach is most commonly found amongst small companies, but at least one major European manufacturer, with an outstanding reputation for the quality and design of its products, also follows this policy and does not directly employ any designers.

In such circumstances, the role of the design manager as a co-ordinator becomes highly important. His main concerns are no longer to do with motivation and leadership – he is now responsible for ensuring the continuing relevance of the externally based design work and for monitoring progress against time and cost budgets. In this respect, the necessary administration may become extremely tedious as Topalian[14] shows in his discussion of the documentation required to keep track of projects – job cards, job files, progress reports etc. Also the design brief assumes even greater importance than in the case of in-house design work where ambiguities or problems may be readily resolved. Once a brief has been issued to an outside design group the scope for amending errors is much reduced. Indeed the brief is likely to form part of the contract between the two parties so it may need to be drawn up with legal precision. The design manager is responsible for this and he or she should also be the focus of communications. If a problem does arise, the design consultant should not have to telephone around the client's company in order to find the answer to a question.

In addition to the advantages already mentioned, one attractive feature of commissioning design work outside the company is that it is often easier to abort unsuccessful projects. The whole business is less personal than where emotionally-saturated design projects inside the company remain in continued existence, even as their prospects become ever more bleak, because everyone has a personal stake and no-one has the heart to 'pull the plug'. As each contract period with the outside designer comes to an end, a cool assessment may be made of the real progress and prospects before a further stage is embarked upon.

As well as the design brief, it may be necessary to provide the outside designer with a copy of the company's design manual, if one exists. This is the best way of conveying technical information such as approved colours, typefaces and logos, all of which are necessary in maintaining the corporate identity of the company. Another form of outside design work is where non-specialist managers in very large organisations have to commission design work on a local basis; for example, in large retailing chains, banks, building societies, and large, multi-plant manufacturing companies. Clearly, it would be impossible for a centrally-based design manager to personally co-ordinate all design projects throughout his company. Instead the work must be delegated to local staff and the design manager's responsibility is to provide technical back-up. In this case, the design manual may provide step-by-step instructions on how to hire designers, assess costings and budgets, prepare a brief, evaluate prototypes or 'mock-ups', choose between alternative design solutions, and so on. Only when a problem arises which is outside the scope of the design manual need reference be made to the design manager. The design manual should be comprehensive enough to indicate when these problems may occur and advise referral within its step-by-step format.

## 4.6 Conclusion

In this chapter, an attempt has been made to highlight the organisational features associated with design work. The most important point is that to design new products, or to modify existing ones, always involves some degree of change. Whatever the scale of this change, reaction to it within the company may well be negative and sometimes will be sufficiently intense to kill off a design project before its outcome can be properly evaluated. This calls for special design management skills to maintain a good working relationship between the design unit and the rest of the company. The form of management practised within the unit is also important and some guidance was given about features to be developed and those that should be discouraged. Finally, the management of design work sub-contracted outside the company was considered; here it was seen that administrative skills are most important.

Together with the issues raised in the preceding chapters of this book, it will now be apparent that the responsibilities of design management can be very wide indeed. As well as a responsibility for planning for design and preparing a product strategy, design management is also concerned with 'picking the winners' – evaluating product ideas – and selecting the right designer for the job within or, from outside the company, or putting together the best design team. The next chapter discusses the venture concept at some length and provides a case study illustration of some of the benefits and limitations of the approach. An interesting insight into the way design relates to other functions in a company is provided by a recent report[15] on the organisation of design in several different companies within the footwear industry. Also, while not dealing specifically with design organisation, Blakstad's case studies[16] highlight more of the problems.

# 5  Case Study: Omega Products –
# An Experiment in Venture
# Management

## 5.1 Introduction

The use of 'venture groups' as a method of organising for design was mentioned in the last chapter but was not discussed in detail. This chapter is entirely devoted to the topic because the experience of the author is that venture management can be a most effective approach to design and new products if handled properly. Unfortunately, in some instances, the method is not successful. It was a failure in the case presented here, which reports actual events although all names have been changed and which also illustrates many aspects of design management not confined to the venture method. Case studies which report failures or problems can be much more informative than those reporting success and this is the reason for including the 'Omega' case. References are also given to several 'successful' cases.

Before presenting the case some general information is given about venture management. In doing this, it is necessary to point out that although industrial venture systems have been devised and implemented for many years, examination of the literature dealing with the concept still shows a lack of consistency of definition. The venture label is freely applied to management styles which differ in important respects. Often, the only common feature is that the object of discussion is an industrial subgroup concerned with the design of new products. In particular, there is a marked failure to distinguish between venture systems in the USA and the quasi-venture systems which tend to operate elsewhere.

## 5.2 Features of Venture Management

The Venture concept is based on the theory that big companies stand a better chance of successfully launching new products or new designs if they can create conditions, devoid of bureaucracy, where the motivations of entrepreneurs can be given full scope.

In essence, venture systems attempt to simulate the incentives and challenges that small businesses present to those who run them, particularly the prospect of rapid self-advancement. Thus, the most general definition of what is meant by the venture concept of organisation is 'the formation of new businesses by tapping existing technical and human resources. It is an innovative form of management that is designed to get away as much as possible from red tape inherent in a large organisation'.[1]

A venture team is usually set up around a manager who is not restrained in his approach to the project by the organisation of the parent company. Typically the manager and team members are young people who have already demonstrated above-average ability. This is an essential feature of venture groups. Simulation of a small business environment is reinforced in the US where it is common for all members of the team to invest substantial amounts of their own funds in addition to the company contribution[2]. It is likely to be the first opportunity team members have to take such a business risk and their endeavours for success and reward can be expected to be of a high level. In the UK, in line with a more conservative business approach, investment by team members is not common. The main incentive is the prospect of early advancement and the opportunity to run a business at an early stage. This difference in approach is very important and will be referred to again.

Although it has been claimed that venture techniques are widely used in many large firms (such as Monsanto, Du Pont and General Electric in the United States[3] and British Oxygen[4] and ICI[5] in the United Kingdom) there is little evidence in the literature of attempts to compare systems and quantify results. Invariably, papers dwell on business successes and make only passing reference to the features of the organisation responsible for achieving the success. However, a useful paper has been published by Hill and Hlavacek[6] which reports on a study of over 100 venture teams in large companies in the United States. By using questionnaires and personal interviews, a number of unique characteristics are described which distinguish venture teams from traditional forms of industrial organisations. A list of these characteristics helps to define more specifically the nature of venture organisations:

- **Organisationally separate** – as Burns and Stalker[7] also noted, the most successful new product ventures are geographically as well as organisationally separate.
- **Multidisciplinary** – the interaction of team members with different skills is considered essential for creativity.
- **Diffusion of authority** – team members are not confined by job descriptions and are free to develop working relationships; team managers are often indistinguishable from other members.
- **Environment of entrepreneurship** – 'free wheeling' atmosphere together with financial or personal commitment by team members.
- **Top management support** – venture team members usually report to managers at the highest level.
- **Market oriented missions** – rather than product oriented, but otherwise broad discretion in method of operation.
- **Flexible life span** – lack of strict deadlines for the accomplishment of tasks or goals.

In his report on a venture project in ICI, Vernon[5] covers all these points. In some cases there is qualification or emphasis which one might expect to distinguish a British study from an American one. For example he tempers the concept of a 'free wheeling' atmosphere with comments about the need for plans to be made carefully and all staff to be 'finance-conscious'. If team members have a personal financial commitment, this problem will be self-regulating, but where it is common, as in British companies, for all finance to be channelled from the parent company, it is necessary to have checks and procedures to ensure spending is kept to reasonable limits.

Unfortunately, this intrusion of bureaucracy, however slight, can seriously endanger the philosophy. Perhaps this is why Vernon stresses the need for the venture manager to create and maintain optimism within the team. Despite this, Vernon presents a generally hierarchical view of venture organisation. In contrast, Hill and Hlavacek stress the need for the leader to be one amongst equals.

## 5.3 A Recent Venture Experiment

The experiment took place in a subsidiary of a large British group which will be referred to as Omega Products. For many years Omega had produced ranges of small to medium volume products. Substantial innovation had occurred after World War II and a number of important and successful products were launched. Most of these were derivatives of existing products and they satisfactorily served to enlarge existing markets and also to create new ones. One major new product was quite radical and established the company in a useful new business. The product was developed outside the company in a project funded jointly by Omega and the 'Customer'.

It is reported that the success of this project resulted from the determination of three forceful personalities – the inventor of the product, a senior manager of Omega and a senior manager of the 'Customer'. The product was highly profitable for a few years but then turnover began to fall.

The decline of this product formed part of a general decline in Omega's fortunes since the mid-1960s. In a ten year period, turnover had decreased in real terms by 25 per cent. With improvements in production processes, employment had been reduced by some 50 per cent at the same time, causing the loss of over 2,000 jobs. Many of the best markets had disappeared and some products had become obsolescent. Those which remained were mainly being sold to stable or declining markets. To a large extent the company's fortunes were dependent upon the success or failure of a handful of major customers to whom much of the production was sold.

During the years of decline, Omega had made some efforts to introduce new products but none had met with commercial success. One reason for this was that the management team had come to be dominated by managers who saw problems in terms of cost cutting and improvement to existing manufacturing processes. The innovative flair which had flourished during the 1950s had been submerged as the products which it created moved into the mature stages of their lives. Many creative individuals had left the company to work elsewhere, or had retired or resigned themselves to grow old with their products.

There is evidence that during the period of decline, expenditure on product innovation was grudging and inadequate. Research and design expenditure in Omega ran at about one third the average level maintained by similar British firms in the industry. In addition to this financial perspective, interviews with members of staff and inspections of written records confirmed the trend. It was found that the design projects which were allowed to start up were under constant attack by critics. They were frequently dismissed as irrelevant even by the most senior members of the company.

In the late 1970's some new senior managers began to make their mark in the company. Amongst a number of changes which took place, was a decision to devote more resources to a programme of new product development. It was decided that the programme would be run on venture lines and a new divison of the company was formed to provide a framework for design projects. This new division was created by the reorganisation of the existing production divisions of the company. See *figures 5.1* and *5.2* for simplified organisation diagrams.

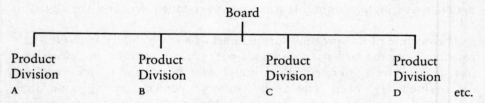

*Figure 5.1  Old Organisation of Omega Products*

It was intended that each venture project would be run as an independent enterprise. Its manager would report straight to the new division's director who, together with the other divisional directors, was a board member. In this way, it was anticipated that decisions about appraisal and finance would be taken speedily and that this high level linkage would ensure general protection from the system.

The grouping of the new ventures with the old division A was an attempt to use the experience built up in that division. The ventures were financially separate with independent budgets and could buy services and goods from division A in the same way as from external sources. As the ventures flourished, it was thought that each would become established as a separate operating division in their own right.

Six months after these structural changes, it was clear that the new ventures were not working as expected. The first of the projects had been run down and most of the staff posted elsewhere. Other projects were failing to prosper and their managers and staff were becoming demoralised. The following six factors were seen to be responsible:

**Inadequate initial screening of projects and lack of marketing awareness.**

Such was the initial enthusiasm of the management of Omega for the venture idea that the first product for development was selected without proper consideration of its potential. It has been claimed[8] that most venture failures arise because neither the product nor the manager is sufficiently outstanding. In too many cases, the product has neither a sufficiently large sales potential nor a big enough profit margin to provide the foundation for an independent business. On the basis of the information available, neither Omega nor the venture groups could have forecast sales or profit with any certainty.

Perhaps even more fundamental was the failure to be sufficiently market-oriented in the selection of projects. Omega was particularly weak in terms of marketing and much previous innovation had failed because technical ingenuity had taken precedence over gaining an understanding of the user's needs. Several excellent products had been devised for which it was eventually found that only insignificant sales could be obtained. This does not mean that results of speculative development work should be ignored. Vernon[5] indicates that the success of the ICI venture operation stemmed from a chance technical discovery; but the starting point was a

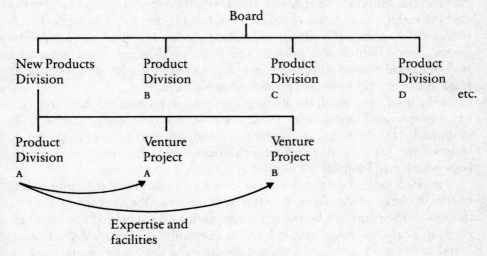

*Figure 5.2 New Organisation of Omega Products*

market analysis and only when an opportunity was identified did design work begin in earnest.

**Lack of commitment by top management.**
Faced with the news of design problems in the first project, the reaction of the management was to take resources away from it. Conversely, when progress and prospects looked good, ever more optimistic targets were set. The point here is that once a potential project has been thoroughly analysed and then selected, the venture group should be insulated from inconsistency. Whilst the company was naturally anxious to see projects succeed, it should have been ready to accept that some – even a majority – might fail and the best chance of success would be assured by steady but distant support.

**Lack of protection from the organisation.**
Very soon after the first venture project was established, the pressure of bureaucracy began to be felt. At the corporate level the Strategic Planning Department decided it would need the venture manager to provide extensive product appraisal information. A lengthy questionnaire was issued which demanded information in great detail about technical and commercial aspects of the project. It was returned for revision several times and the estimates which it contained began to be regarded as facts.

More disturbing, the simple predictions, acknowledged to be 'guesstimates', upon which the project had been established, were increased without good reason during the process, so that the project appeared to grow more attractive and expectations were raised.

At the divisional level, the Buying Department monitored the purchases of material and equipment made by the venture team members. It complained that, through inexperience, some high prices were being paid. It insisted on the use of 'correct procedure' and the result was much paperwork and long delays instead of immediate deliveries.

The effect of these actions was to divert and dilute the entrepreneurial energy of the team members. A better 'selling job' of the venture concept to the rest of the company by the management may have helped but, short of geographical separation, it is unlikely that established service departments could have stood aside, perhaps to be eclipsed if the new venture grew to success.

## Reluctance to give venture manager freedom of action.

The problems concerning purchasing have already been mentioned. There was also a tendency for staff to be appointed to the projects who were not the choice of the venture manager. In the area of finance, although budgets were agreed and allocated, the venture manager was required to obtain authorisation for even relatively small expenditures. The effect of these interferences and restrictions was to blunt the enthusiasm of the manager and his team.

## Tendency for mechanistic forms of operation to be created within the venture group.

The chosen venture managers had gained their experience largely within the parent company, and it is not surprising, therefore, that they tended to develop their groups along traditional lines. Hannan[3], Gardner[4] and Hill and Hlavacek[6] all suggest that an informal organisation with uninhibited communications is the ideal form for innovative groups. The groups set up by Omega soon showed the manifestations of an emerging hierarchy with the grading of offices, competition for appointment of secretaries, and a general growth of paperwork. Inevitably, preoccupation with these elements led to reduced vitality in the real work of the project.

## Lack of real incentive for team members to succeed.

In this venture experiment there was no question of financial investment by the team members to be followed by the prospect of high reward when the project became a success. The main incentive lay in the suggestion that if all went well and a good business was created, then the participants would assume positions at a much higher level than they could otherwise have expected. However, another possibility which was stated was that as the project developed, it would be 'grafted' on to an existing operation and come under the control of an experienced senior line manager. Although this case study is not about venture management in a 'pure' form, it gives an insight into the organisational problems than can occur when a company attempts to simulate a venture approach in order to encourage success in design or other innovative work.

## 5.4 Conclusion

In general, appraisal of the potential of the venture concept is made difficult because the published accounts tend to be concerned with projects that have been commercially successful. It is felt that this case study may help to increase understanding of the venture concept by presenting information about an unsuccessful attempt to introduce it within a large UK company and by diagnosing organisational factors that may render a venture group impotent.

The unsuccessful Omega experiment highlights a number of essential features which are necessary if a venture exercise is to achieve its objectives. The essential features which were seen to be absent from Omega can be summarised as:
  - Proper understanding of products and markets.
  - Consistent top management support.
  - Protection from large company bureaucracy.
  - Venture manager's freedom of action.
  - Free wheeling informal operation.
  - Real incentives for team members.

The discussion in section 5.2 indicated the importance of the difference between the operation of the venture concept in the United States and elsewhere. The original concept was tied up fundamentally with financial participation by team members as well as by the parent organisation and third parties. This element of personal commitment is not usual outside the United States and was not evident in this case study; consequently the results obtained by such 'quasi-venture' groups may be quite different from those obtained by real venture groups.

It is dangerous to generalise from a single case but the Omega exericse suggests that two aspects are especially important:

**The need for geographical separation** – many of the problems encountered by Omega were aggravated because the groups had to operate within an existing company location. This made it too easy for the established bureaucracy to interfere and for conspicuous entrepreneurial action to be criticised.

**The need for real incentives for team members** – whether this is by bonus payments, equity participation or some other means, the requirement is that there should be the prospect of relatively considerable personal gain. Indication of rapid promotion is not, in itself, sufficient incentive.

# 6 Managing Design: Practical Issues

## 6.1 Introduction

In earlier chapters, attention was directed to some of the preliminary decisions and investigations which are required before serious work can begin on designing new or improved products. The discussion was concerned with the examination of market opportunities for new products, and also the state of resources within the firm that could be used to create them. In particular, the nature of design departments was explored, with attention given to the facilities needed by them and the special organisational problems which can arise. This chapter continues the examination by reviewing the main aspects of design work and by then attempting to evaluate the extent of designers' responsibilities for features such as cost, quality and compatibility.

## 6.2 Product Specifications and Project Briefs

The starting point for a new product should always be some kind of 'specification'. Depending on the complexity or scale of the project, the specification may be little more than a rough sketch and a few notes.

However, for a new product such as a motor vehicle, the specification may run to many volumes and describe in precise terms the multitude of parameters which must be observed. Such a document might take several months, or even years, to prepare and will be based on extensive market investigations and internal policy deliberations. Generally though, specifications should be as simple as possible and should be presented in such a way that designers are allowed maximum discretion. There is little point in employing creative design staff if freedom of action is then restricted by excessive direction.

The essential information which ought to be provided by the specification may be summarised as follows:

- **Exact type of product to be designed** – described in terms of existing alternative productions if available, or in terms of the **functions required** if the product is a totally new concept.
- **Major technical requirements** – such as speed of operation, maximum and minimum dimensions that can be allowed, performance levels required, etc.
- **Styling requirements** – general nature of appearance, shapes and colours preferred, carrying capacity, arrangement of major features, etc.
- **Operational requirements** – size of controls, forces required to operate, safety features, compatibility with operator's dimensions or other items of equipment, etc.
- **Cost constraints** – target selling prices or production costs of the product, requirements regarding maintenance and service cost levels if relevant, and operating costs, etc.
- **Special requirements** – for example, 'need for product to be safe for use by small children'.

Exactly where the responsibility lies for preparing the specification will vary from company to company (see chapter 7). Frequently, it is put together by representatives of the major functions perhaps through the mechanism of a 'new product committee'. Sometimes the specification is compiled by a senior executive or by a specialist consultant. Regardless of the way it is put together, the final version should be understood, approved and supported by top management. The specification for a new product determines, at least in part, the company's future achievements and prospects; for this reason its importance should not be undermined by indifferent management attitudes.

The product specification usually forms a part of a larger document, the project brief (or 'design brief'). Success in design work is not dependent upon simply achieving a final version of the new product which satisfies the specification. It is also important that the work is completed within a period of time and at a cost which will enable the product to stand a chance of becoming a commercial success. Information about the time and cost constraints is a major element of the project brief.

The duration of a design project may be important in marketing terms – if a project lasts too long, competitors may become firmly established in the market and overall prospects for the new product will be greatly diminished. Another consequence of a late project is that total design costs will increase which, coupled with a delayed product launch (and hence delayed sales income), may push the whole project into irretrievable financial deficit as *figure 6.1* shows.

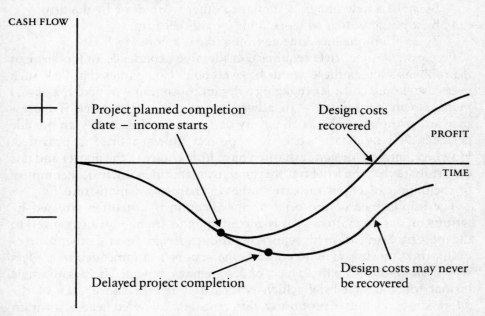

*Figure 6.1  Effect of Time Delay on Cash Flow of Design Project*

If design costs are running at a high level, a very short delay indeed may transform the prospects for the new product from good to doubtful. Worse still, if the increased debt caused by the delay cannot be covered by the company then bankruptcy may be the inevitable result. In recent years, spectacular failures in the aircraft industry have received much attention but many other companies of more modest scale have suffered similar disastrous consequences as a result of their inabilities to sustain the losses caused by out-of-control design projects.

To avoid these problems, great care must go into planning design projects and then preparing briefs which give clear guidance on all constraints, but particularly on time and cost. This is simply stated but in practice is not so easy to achieve. There have been attempts to analyse the discrepancies which arise in many projects between original cost estimates and the eventual outcome. These have led to various rules-of-thumb for calculating the actual final cost of a project, such as multiplying the first estimate:

- By $\pi/2$ if a new design is similar to other work done by the firm.
- By $\pi$ if it is similar to work done by another firm.
- By $2\pi$ if no-one has done anything like it before.[1]

Preparing design briefs requires considerable experience and judgement if problems such as these are to be overcome. Companies that lack such expertise should consider engaging a design consultant – or better, a design management consultant – to advise on preparing the brief. To press forward without a brief at all is very dangerous and generally an outside designer will not start work on a project unless a brief is provided. However, internal design staff often have little choice in the matter and it is unfortunate that the briefings they are given are often unclear, incomplete or even non-existent as the case studies in chapter 7 demonstrate.

The importance of the brief or specification is not often stressed by writers on design matters so it is encouraging to see high priority given to the topic by Corfield[2] in his report on product design. Several other sources of information such as Watts[3] and Leslie[4] can be recommended to readers who wish to follow up this aspect of design management. There is no single format for a design brief which is ideal for all situations; each of the references given above proposes a different set of detailed headings within which the brief should be prepared. However, there is general agreement that the main areas of concern must always be product performance (covered by the specification), time and cost.

## 6.3 The Design Operation

The designer's task is to seek workable solutions which satisfy the requirements of the specification. Typically this entails the sketching of basic ideas followed by modifications and the insertion of more and more detail until a complete solution to the problem is achieved. It is far outside the scope of this book to analyse in detail the whole practice of design. However, although the reader is directed for further information to the wide literature on the topic – a sample of which forms part of the list of references[5,6,7,8] – there are a number of points which can be usefully made here.

For example, it is interesting to consider the general nature of design work. In most projects there is both a *technical* content and an *artistic* content. Cursory examination of household products will confirm this. Electrical appliances, tools, items of furniture, fabrics, cutlery, floor coverings – all have involved technical design work in some measure to achieve performance, rigidity, durability, safety etc. Similarly, an artistic input will have been involved, particularly in the case of furnishings and other products which are purchased largely on the basis of appearance. For many products, technical features are well understood and the job of the designer is to apply the most suitable technology to a particular problem. To do this efficiently, the designer needs to receive appropriate technical training but, equally important, must have access to up-to-date information. The responsibility of the design manager is to ensure that both these requirements are met, the first by training and staff development, the second by the provision of technical information systems within the firm and by encouraging designers to explore new technological developments outside the firm.

Similar comments can be made about the artistic aspects of design. Perhaps the most important point that managers need to grasp is that artistic aspects of product design are not necessarily of minor importance. It is true that, in the past, some products have competed on technical strengths with little interest given to appearance or other artistic features – for example engineering machine tools, commercial vehicles and many consumer products. Now, with competing manufacturers able to achieve similar high levels of technical quality and performance, it is often the artistic features of products which determine success in the market place.

The artistic features of products need to be considered throughout the design process and not just at the final stage. Where projects are of such a small scale that only individual designers are involved, they have to pay regard to both technical and artistic considerations. In larger companies, with more extensive design operations, there will be some designers who will be technical specialists (the 'design engineers' perhaps) and others who will concentrate on artistic aspects (the 'industrial designers' or 'stylists'). Projects must be tackled by both on a collaborative basis from the beginning. A sequential approach of first tackling the technical problems and then handing over to the stylist to 'finish the job' does not lead to consistently good results.

In addition to these aspects of design work, there are two other areas of importance. These may be called the *ergonomic* and *economic* considerations of design. They are often seen as minor components in the overall design process, but increasingly they are developing as important specialisms.

A 'good' ergonomic design is one which is totally satisfactory to the user in terms of the way it 'suits' the human body. For example, a motor car with excellent visibility, well-positioned controls and easily adjustable seats is ergonomically good. However, step-ladders which easily trap fingers and ironing boards which cause backache are examples of ergonomically bad designs. For many products it is a straightforward matter to ensure that the design will be convenient in use; all that is required is an awareness that dimensions, material choice, layout and so on must all be appropriate for normal conditions of use. Where there is doubt, or when the design area is an unfamiliar one, satisfactory ergonomic design can be achieved only by studying directly the requirements of users. This may involve the firm in a programme of tests and measurements using a sample of subjects selected to represent the range of characteristics relevant to the design problem in hand. Such work may best be left to specialists where ergonomic considerations are especially important or if sensitive issues need to be investigated.

However, in many cases a few simple checks by the design department may be all that is required to determine whether, say, a range of four products rather than three is necessary to satisfy all likely users, or whether a particular layout of controls is readily understandable. It is much better that a little time and expense should be devoted to the direct examination of users' characteristics at the design stage, than to allow problems to be identified by the customer after purchase, possibly leading to early re-design or even withdrawal of the product.

For many firms, economic considerations in design work are confined to ensuring that eventual costs of manufacture will be sufficiently low to enable the product to be sold at a price which will allow a reasonable operating profit. It is clearly one of the designer's main responsibilities to avoid any unnecessary costs in his work and this will be considered in greater detail later. However, it is often imperative that adequate consideration is given to other economic aspects of products apart from just manufacturing cost and selling price.

Products which consume fuel may need to be designed to be as efficient as possible. In the wake of the recent escalation in the price of all kinds of fuel, many customers are anxious about the running costs of the products they are buying. So it is found that even products like televisions and refrigerators, which previously might have been considered 'negligible' consumers of power, are now judged by their efficiency. To achieve efficiency, the designer may have to restrict the number of features that can be incorporated in the product or he may have to propose some other kind of compromise, perhaps affecting quality or performance.

Another 'economic' concern of customers is the level of maintenance expenditure that may be required. This expenditure can be greatly affected by actions at the design stage. If components are designed so that they can be easily replaced by the customer without specialist knowledge or equipment, then the product will be much cheaper to maintain than if expert attention is required. Maintenance costs will be even less if parts are designed so that they last for the life of the product. But this may involve higher standards of quality and consequently higher selling prices for the product. Thus a balance may have to be sought between purchase price, maintenance expenditure and runnings costs in order to offer the customer an attractive 'overall deal'. A good designer or design team will be able to explore these problems and devise appropriate solutions. However, ultimately it is a matter of company policy to decide how the economic considerations of products should be resolved. If, for example, the aim is to achieve the lowest possible selling price in the market the design of the product may reflect this by using cheap materials and production methods which may then dictate a subsequent high level of maintenance expenditure.

## 6.4 The Value Engineering Concept

The real skill in design lies in the ability to satisfy simultaneously all the demands of both the firm which manufactures the product and the customer who buys it. The basic needs of the firm are minimum cost of production coupled with maximum profit – which depends very largely on the attractiveness of the product to the customer. In competitive markets, the customer's decision to purchase one firm's product rather than another is based on 'value'. Not just 'value for money' or 'economic value', but a concept of 'total value' comprising an adequate measure of all the attributes that the customer feels he requires. Broadly speaking these attributes include those aspects of design already mentioned: the technical, artistic, ergonomic and economic aspects.

The term 'Value Engineering' is sometimes used to describe a philosophy of design where the aim is to provide maximum value for the customer at minimum cost to the producer.[9] Value Engineering emphasises the need to understand exactly what the customer requires and to preserve this from the beginning to the end of the design process. But it also emphasises the need for minimum cost and in order to achieve this advocates the use of certain techniques of critical appraisal, particularly at the later stages of the design process.[10]

These techniques are described in chapter 9 which is concerned with the need for the periodic re-design of existing products to improve the maximum value/minimum cost relationship. The final stage in the design of a new product should be to view it as an existing product and to apply these techniques (of 'Value Analysis') to ensure that the best possible design has indeed been achieved given the circumstances prevailing. As will be seen later, the Value Engineering/Value Analysis approach introduces several special features into the design operation including the direct involvement of non-designers, the encouragement of multi-disciplinary teamwork, and the thorough examination of every component of the design to ensure both that its function is necessary and that it is being achieved in the most cost-effective manner.

## 6.5 The Development Operation

It has been stated already that the designer's task is to seek solutions which satisfy the requirements of the specification. Usually a final design cannot be achieved without a good deal of testing of ideas and experimental comparisons of alternative solutions. Hence, design units are often supported by some kind of 'development' facility – basically a workshop or laboratory where test-pieces can be made and subjected to whatever examination may be required.

Design and development proceeds hand in hand. During the early stages of the design programme, the demand on development may be for information about material strengths or corrosion resistance, for example. Later, when this information has been used and the design of the product has proceeded to the point where a general layout has been achieved, individual components may be built by the development section and tested to assess properties or performance. In the light of the results obtained, the design can be changed as necessary to meet the standards demanded by the specification. Eventually, a final version of the new product will be built and tested, typically to examine features like reliability, durability, safety and general performance.

Depending on the scale of the product being designed, the development effort may be concerned with scale-models or full-size models. Where possible, full-size tests should always be encouraged because 'scale-up' results usually involve some error; obviously this is not always feasible when dealing with products like aircraft, ships or similar objects. Similarly, it should be remembered that full-sized models (sometimes called 'prototypes') which have been made using 'one-off' techniques rather than mass production methods may exhibit features different from those of the finished product. Consequently, the final activity of the design operation should be to examine the product as soon as the production process has been set up. Some unexpected features may be discovered which must be rectified before large scale production commences. Sometimes quite major problems are encountered at this stage as a result of lack of co-operation between production and design during earlier stages of the project. In chapter 4 it was noted that relationships between these departments may be difficult because of the differences in organisational styles and objectives. Nevertheless, it is essential that production is involved in design decisions as they are made.[11] Failure to do so is a recipe for disaster – years of design effort may be wasted if assumptions are made about production matters without checking the true facts.

The co-operation of production managers is also needed to enable realistic design trials to be carried out. Often actual production equipment has to be used to test ideas or to form components for prototype trials; few firms can afford to duplicate highly specialised production equipment, so time has to be set aside for experimental work. This can be acutely irritating to production managers who are usually judged by their ability to reach output targets and they may well resist or obstruct design projects. The answer lies in ensuring that capacity lost during development exercises is properly 'credited' to the production department. Once again, it can be seen that what is needed is a proper understanding of the nature of new product work by top management, together with a firm commitment once a project is underway.

Another reason why close co-operation is essential between design and production functions is that product design and process design are increasingly to be found proceeding hand in hand. This is particularly noticeable in complex manufacturing businesses like those in the motor industry. Widescale adoption of new materials, for example, is accompanied by the introduction of new manufacturing processes and assembly techniques. Frequently, the technologies of both the product and the process are at the same stage of development and joint programmes make sound economic and organisational sense.

## 6.6 Legal Aspects of Design

This is a suitable point to draw attention to some of the legal considerations which are of concern to designers. Legal issues may arise at any point in the design cycle. When planning projects and preparing specifications, it is important that potential legal problems are considered and accounted for. There may be specific laws which regulate the scope of activity in certain fields; for example, laws restricting the use of potentially dangerous materials such as asbestos or explosives. The details of these laws are likely to be well-known to companies already well-established in the field, but newcomers will need to do some research to assess the scope of any restrictions. Details should then be recorded in the project brief.

Once practical work has been started, problems may arise in connection with patents or other forms of design protection. Sometimes a favoured solution to a design problem may be one which uses, or partly uses, an existing idea which has been developed by someone else and is now subject to legal protection. In such a case, the question arises as to whether it is desirable or possible to acquire the rights to use the idea. This course of action may be expensive and it is very rare that only one solution is possible – either a different solution may be found or, using the legally protected idea as a starting point, an improved version of it may be devised which falls outside the scope of the legal protection.

As design projects progress, decisions may need to be taken about seeking legal protection for the results that have been achieved. Also, before any product is released onto the market, very great care must be taken to ensure that it will not violate any consumer legislation, that it is safe in use and unlikely to give rise to any action for negligent design. Hence, there are two broad areas which need to be considered; aspects of the law which are, on the one hand, to do with the rights of those involved in creating new products, and, on the other, concern the rights of those who buy and use these products.

## Rights of Designers, Inventors and Companies

In order to encourage innovation, most countries provide various forms of legal protection of ownership and exploitation to the originators of new products or new designs[12,13]. Most managers are familiar with the concept of patent protection – in effect a monopoly of manufacture, trade and use granted (for up to 20 years in the United Kingdom) in respect of a particular novelty of function. The procedure for obtaining a United Kingdom patent is not unduly complex nor expensive in terms of fees charged by the Patent Office. However, the degree of protection which the patent will provide ultimately depends upon the thoroughness with which the 'claims' are presented. To ensure that 'loopholes' that might be used by competitors are not overlooked, most companies use specialist lawyer-engineers (patent agents) to manage patent applications. Large companies may employ their own specialists, but most firms will use independent consultants. Either way may involve considerable expense, even more so if patents are being sought in a number of countries where translators and foreign agents will have to be engaged.

In view of this, and the fact that around three years normally elapses between the initial application and eventual granting of a patent (during which time no real protection exists), the number of occasions where a patent is appropriate is relatively small – only in those cases where a long and lucrative life for the product is envisaged.

Unfortunately, designers and their companies often see the accumulation of a larger number of patents as a measure of achievement. In fact, the granting of patents in no way guarantees any commercial success and may even detract from it if the pursuit of patents becomes an end in itself rather than a means. However, there are circumstances where patents may be highly beneficial. In these cases, apart from the initial application,[14] all stages in the procedure should be handled by a competent specialist.

While a patent protects the function of an object, usually it does not give any protection to its appearance. Yet distinctive appearance is often a major factor in the success of a product. The law recognises ownership of product designs in the same sort of way that it recognises ownership of other artistic creations such as music, paintings, books and plays. Copyright automatically protects the distinctive appearance of a firm's products; legal action to prevent infringement and to recover damages may be brought if copying or imitation occurs. Such action may not be easy where the source of the infringement is overseas, or where there is difficulty in proving ownership of the original design.

The latter problem may be minimised by registration of the design, as soon as it is conceived, with the Designs Registry of the Patent Office. The procedure for doing this is simple although, as in the case of patent procedures, reference to an appropriate specialist, or at least an authoritative text,[15] is strongly advised.

## Rights of Users of Products

There has been a considerable increase in the scope of consumer legislation in recent years, both in the United Kingdom and elsewhere. Many of these laws directly affect the actions of designers, for example where minimum standards of performance are specified or where levels of quality are prescribed. Of particular importance is the question of product liability[16] – the trend in many countries is towards the view that consumers should be entitled to compensation for losses caused as a result of the defective design of products. In some cases, individual designers and managers as well as their companies may be held responsible if negligence or wilful malpractice is proven.[17]

The basic concern is that of product safety. There are three reasons[18] why a product may become defective. The most common is a design mistake which means that every unit produced will share the fault; if the fault is very serious, all the products which have been sold may have to be recalled. The second reason is a manufacturing error which is only likely to affect a small number of products. Finally, products may become unsafe if used inappropriately and failure to warn of the danger of this could leave a company open to legal action. This final area is probably the greatest problem of all, since it may be very difficult for the designers or manufacturers of products to foresee all possible methods of abuse or misuse.

The existence of an EEC draft directive on product liability, and the growing influence of the various consumer lobbies, tends to make companies extremely cautious about safety issues. Recent history shows that many well-known companies have been involved in recall campaigns to withdraw products which often have only a slight safety problem. Considering the adverse effects this course of action may have on the corporate image of a company, it is clear that the problem is one which is being taken very seriously indeed.

Given that most product defects arise out of mistakes at the design stage, this is where greatest effort to avoid the problem should be concentrated. One check that should be included before the new product is launched is a review of the latest relevant legal requirements to ensure that all are satisfied by the design as it stands. Wherever possible, designs should be finalised in compliance with officially recognised state-of-the-art standards[19]; failure to do this in future will certainly restrict export sales to countries with tougher product liability laws. Even in the United Kingdom, voluntary certification and compliance with officially endorsed standards will become more important as a defence against actions for damages arising out of defective design.

One further design issue connected with the question of product liability is the need to 'finger-print' products or component parts. When a design defect does occur, it is important that the exact location and extent of the problem can be determined. If this is not possible, a company may be involved in a very wide recall exercise involving a majority of perfectly sound products. During the design process, potentially troublesome components should be identified and systems devised so that records are available of the origin and end-use of these components. Clearly, in the case of a product like a motor car containing several hundred safety-critical components the task is very large. However this is put into perspective when compared with the alternative of having to recall perhaps hundreds of thousands of vehicles should a serious fault develop.

Consumer law is complex and is changing rapidly and no attempt can be made here to present even a summary of all relevant legislation. All that can be said is that it is important for design managers to be aware that such legislation exists and that they should obtain qualified advice about the extent to which their activities may be affected by it.

## 6.7 Designing for Production

In carrying out their work, designers have many responsibilities both within the firm and outside. The need to comply with the requirements of consumer legislation has already been discussed. Designers must also ensure that their work satisfies customers' needs – that products work well, are attractive, have acceptable dimensions, do not make too much noise, are easy to maintain, and so on.

Within the company, designers must aim to satisfy the requirements of many different functions. Finance will demand a product that will enable an acceptable return on investment to be achieved. Marketing will expect a product that will complement the existing range and will allow the fulfilment of operational plans. Production will be concerned with cost, time and quality considerations, and also with ensuring that the new product will be compatible with existing systems. Good design practice means accommodating all these demands and this is the basis of the 'Value Engineering concept' discussed earlier in this chapter. It cannot be stressed too strongly how dangerous it is to aim consistently to satisfy only certain demands – say, those of the production department – whilst ignoring others. Examples of products as dissimilar as motorcycles and 'real ale' illustrate the folly of misjudging consumer taste

Having stressed the need for a balanced approach to design, the rest of this chapter will investigate the demands made by production departments upon product designers. The reason for concentrating on this topic stems from the writer's belief that the relationship between design and production is frequently misunderstood, despite the fact that is is highly important. In the many companies which provide common, widely available products, the key element in success is highly efficient manufacture. To a large extent, this efficiency depends in turn on a sound working relationship between design and production departments.

## 6.8 Designer's Responsibility for Quality, Time and Cost of Production

As far as quality is concerned, the designer must aim to achieve the standards demanded by the specification, but at the same time not exceed the capabilities of the production department. This may not be an easy task because the determinants of quality are frequently difficult to identify. The specification may be explicit enough in the terms in which quality of the new product is described – for example, in terms of minimum acceptable working life, adequacy of performance and other aspects. The designer must decide how these are affected by features of the production process, as well as by his choice of materials, particular design solutions, etc. If he knows that a certain manufacturing operation can only achieve, say, very poor dimensional tolerances, he must decide whether such an operation can be used for the new product. If it cannot, he must devise an alternative solution.

In many companies, manufacturing quality standards are set down in written form in manuals or data sheets. These standards may take account of the equipment and skills available in the firm; they may also specify the grades and types of material that can be used for different applications. In such firms, the responsibility of the designer is to be familiar with these standards and to work within them. Where no published standards exist, the designer must discover them for himself. This can only be done by thoroughly understanding the production system, the skill level of the workforce, and the nature of existing products.

Time and cost of production are similar in that both need to be kept to a minimum and the design of any new product should reflect this. Further, these two aspects are usually interdependent, for example, a cheap grade of material may require slow machining speeds and thus generate high labour costs; a simple design solution rather than a complex one may allow unskilled labour to be used rather than highly-paid skilled workers and may reduce production times as well.

Clearly the skill of the designer can have substantial impact on production times and costs. It is a skill which is certainly influenced by aptitude, training and experience, but it depends also upon close co-operation between production staff and designers and upon a 'sense of value' within the firm as a whole. There are many possibilities to be explored and many 'trade-offs' to be evaluated in achieving the goal of minimum product costs. As an indication of the scope of the topic some examples are given below of measures that should be considered at the design stage:

**Labour costs** can be minimised by:
– Taking the skill out of each operation.
– Reducing the number of operations.
– Reducing the time of essential operations that cannot be eliminated.
– Eliminating the possibility of errors during manufacture.

**Material costs** can be minimised by:
– Using as few components as possible.
– Choosing component dimensions to make economic use of raw material;
– Using the cheapest materials consistent with quality standards.
– Specifying existing materials as far as possible.

**Equipment costs** can be minimised by:
– Specifying existing equipment rather than new equipment.
– Designing jigs, tools etc. to facilitate economic production.
– Selecting cheap rather than expensive processes.

In general, costs can be minimised by adopting policies of *standardisation*. For example, the use of existing components rather than designing new ones is a form of standardisation. Not only can this save the designer's time, but it also means that longer production runs will be possible and that larger material orders can be placed, both of which lead to economies. Even if an existing component cannot be used in the new product, it may still be possible to choose an existing material rather than a new one so that purchasing economies and stockholding savings can be achieved.

An awareness of the benefits of standardisation may lead to a similar awareness of the value of *specialisation*. In large design departments it may be advantageous if there is some specialisation of tasks. Standardisation of components and materials will be encouraged if individual designers are able to develop expertise in particular areas. Another aspect of specialisation is where excellence in manufacturing skills is recognised and exploited by designers. Such excellence may be within the firm or outside; some highly successful companies have a policy of always specifying the most reliable or economical supplies of components, regardless of source. Designers should always recommend the use of bought-in parts from specialised suppliers if these really do represent the best value obtainable.

Standardisation and specialisation are both concerned with the *reduction of variety* in design and in manufacture, a third form of which is *simplification*. This is concerned with the avoidance of unnecessary complexity in either the design of products or the ways they are made. Most of the approaches listed above for achieving minimum cost are examples of simplification.

Minimum cost of production, like many other aspects of design work, can only be a goal for the designer for a perfect design can never be achieved – there is never enough time or knowledge available and some subsequent improvement is always possible. 'Good' design is that which consistently yields better-than-average results for the firm. Although the doctrines of standardisation, specialisation and simplification are by no means new or unfamiliar, they are a proven key to the achievement of design which is 'good' from a production viewpoint. Thus it is important that production managers and others, as well as designers, should appreciate the benefits that can result from a preoccupation with variety reduction in all its forms.

## 6.9 Need for New Products to be Compatible with Existing Production

Designing to appropriate standards of quality and minimum levels of cost and time are certainly major responsibilities of designers. Where new production facilities are being created specifically for the new product, these may be the only responsibilities. But where existing production systems are to be used, there are other factors which must be considered before the design is completed to ensure that the new product will be compatible.[20] This is a topic which is covered in few texts yet, in this writer's experience, is perhaps the greatest cause of friction between production managers and designers.

Compatibility must be achieved with the production process and with existing products. This involves ensuring that design features are appropriate to existing methods and that they do not cause disruptions. An extreme example of non-compatibility might be where a product was designed to be built using equipment not present in the factory. Another example could be where manufacture of the new product would cause overloading of a particular process.

The key to the problem lies in the designer's knowledge of the production set-up. Many designers have practical experience of production and fully understand the limitations and capabilities that they must work within. Unfortunately, there are also many who do not have this experience and, quite simply, do not appreciate the systems that they are supposed to be designing for. When this situation arises, the responsible production manager will adopt a constructive attitude and ensure that the design department is provided with a detailed picture of the true nature of his department. This information should cover:

– Type of production system (e.g. batch, line, etc).
– Processes available (e.g. casting, welding, etc).
– Handling and storage facilities.
– Nature of the workforce and skills available.
– List of preferred sub-contractors and their skills.
– Breakdown of current products.
– Utilisation of processes and machines.
– Quality limits and inspection procedures.
– Materials used and stockholding facilities.

Only with this basic knowledge can designers hope to achieve compatibility; the more complete the knowledge, the better the chances of a smooth start-up of production. It may be useful to have a 'check list of compatibility questions' so that the designer can satisfy himself he has attended to all contentious points. Three basic questions are important:

**Is the new design compatible in terms of existing manufacturing technology?**
– Are existing batch/flow line systems satisfactory? If not what degree of modification is required?
– Is the proposed volume of production compatible with existing volumes?
– Will the new design demand new standards of quality?
– Will changed demands on machines affect the plant maintenance system?

**Is the new design compatible in terms of labour requirements?**
– Are existing skills adequate? If not, is it feasible to demand different skills from those which already exist?
– What about the pattern of working? Does the new design involve a change to existing shift work arrangements?
– How might the new design affect the operation of incentive and payments schemes?

**Is the new design compatible in terms of control?**
– Will existing production control methods be satisfactory?
– Can existing costing procedures be adopted?
– Will new methods of checking quality be required? Will the frequency of inspection be significantly different?
– Are existing material control and handling systems adequate?

Each production system is unique and has special problems so designers must draw up their own checklist of 'compatibility parameters'. It would be misleading to attempt to present a generalised review of parameters. Statements like 'operation cycle times tend to be short in line systems and long in batch systems' are not helpful to designers, and in many cases systems of production are neither 'line' nor 'batch' but a hybrid of the two.

The ideas expressed in the last few pages around the theme 'designing for production' will not appeal to all designers or production specialists. In many, perhaps most, companies in the United Kingdom there is an assumption that production departments should adapt to whatever demands are made. 'It is the job of Design to dream up the ideas and of Production to make them work' sums up a common attitude. In fact, what frequently happens is that the ideas do not work and a great deal of wasted energy is expended. Both production managers and design managers are jealous of their own specialisms and may see co-operation as a threat to autonomy. This is an attitude that can be seen in other departments too, and is reflected in the highly segmented way in which many companies organise themselves. The message for top management is that successful innovation must be a major objective and that it is the responsibility not only of designers, but of all functions in the organisation.

## 6.10 Conclusion

The aim of this chapter was to bring together the major practical issues which are encountered in design work. The range of issues is an indication of the breadth of the design manager's responsibility – from purely internal requirements such as achieving compatibility between new products and existing manufacturing systems to the international scope of product liability legislation. It would be unrealistic to try to draw a conclusion about which issues are the most important for this will vary from company to company. However, the current trend is for greater emphasis to be placed on aspects such as cost and variety reduction, compatibility and inter-changeability, and compliance with laws and standards. The key to achieving success in these respects is the preparation of a comprehensive product specification as part of an effective project brief.

# 7 Product Specifications: Theory and Practice

## 7.1 Introduction

Until a few years ago, it was not uncommon to find that the design of a product and its subsequent manufacture was the responsibility of a single individual. The designer was expected to have a sufficiently broad background to be able to create sound, functional products capable of economic manufacture at the required quantity level[1]. Even today this remains true in some smaller firms, although increasing diversity of skills and technologies usually dictates wider participation in some form. The rapid growth in new materials, technical inventions and higher performance limits has increased the complexity of the design process. Similarly, countless advances in manufacturing technology have been introduced. The combined effect has been to encourage the formation of separate design and production specialisms in all but the very smallest companies. In order to achieve optimum design results, effective collaboration between these specialisms is crucial; yet this aspect has been largely neglected.

In an attempt to improve this state of knowledge, a research project organised by the author is examining the design/production relationship in a number of manufacturing companies. The firms participating in the study are of small or medium size (100 to 1000 employees approximately) and batch manufacturing systems predominate. The relationship between design and production is being explored by means of a number of 'critical issues' such as the role of product specifications and project briefs, skills deployment, variety reduction procedures, modification procedures, etc. This chapter draws on the part of the research concerned with the preparation of the product specification and will concentrate on information gained on this topic from the observation of four companies.

## 7.2 Central Role of the Product Specification

Any examination of the design process is likely to arrive at the conclusion that success is not entirely dependent upon organisational structure or administrative practice. It is possible to point to many industrial design processes which apparently exhibit every desirable manifestation of logical good-practice and efficiently generate products which are sound from a technical point of view, but which are consistently unsuccessful because they fail to achieve acceptance by customers. In such cases it is likely that the defect resides in the firm's perception of its relationship with markets and individual customers – an inability to recognise that the success of a business is determined by satisfying customers' aspirations, not just by offering technical competence in products which are assumed to be satisfactory but which may be outmoded or inappropriate in other ways[2].

Ideally, a design project should be conceived, and a product specification formulated, in the light of extensive marketing data and preferably with the participation of the customer as well as internal interests. Thereafter, action should be taken to review and refine the specification as improved information becomes available. What mitigates against this vital practice is a widespread tendency to view the design process as a series of successive steps or stages. Thus even a distinguished recent contribution[3] perpetuates the problem by analysing design operations in this step-wise manner. Other writers take a similar approach; whilst the terminology employed to describe the steps may vary, the descriptions are essentially the same[4]. It is the exception[5] rather than the rule to find anything more than a passing reference to the importance of effective feedback of information or the development of vital interrelationships.

This suggests that, in many cases, the product specification will be constructed inadequately in the first place, and then that the essential process of redefining the specification will be omitted as well. This has consequences other than the obvious one of ultimate failure to satisfy customers. Since the specification should constitute a major part of the project brief – the master plan for both the design project and the new product – it may, if poorly researched and constructed, fail to supply the necessary guidance required for the effective organisation of the design work. In particular, the interfaces between design and other functions in the company assume vital importance at certain stages in the design process.

For example, the nature of the relationship between design and production departments has been seen both to greatly assist and seriously obstruct the overall design effort[6]. Unless an intelligent specification has been prepared and its central role is acknowledged, the chances will be greatly increased that indecision or conflict will predominate and lead to substandard results.

In order to avoid the problem of an inadequate specification, it is important to get away from the step-by-step concept of design. The simple but inescapable view that all design must start with the customer and finish with the customer, has to be established and reinforced[7]. This can be done by recognising that design projects are both cyclic and interactive in nature (See *figures 1.4 and 7.1*) and that while the design department is in the main

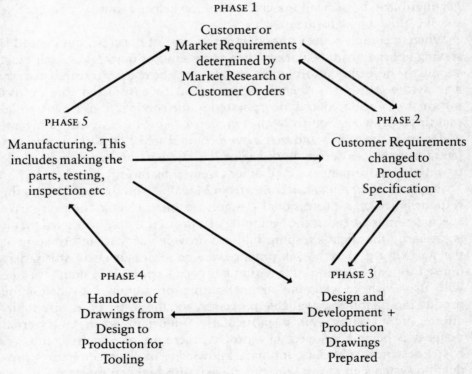

Figure 7.1  *A Diagrammatic Representation of the Key Stages Involved in a Typical Design Project*

stream of translating ideas into products desired by the customers, it should be only one of many participants in the design process.

## 7.3 Compiling Specifications

The initiation of a design project may occur in one of several ways. Most straightforward is the case where a customer makes a direct request for a new product. This may range in form from a vague spoken request to a submission of requirements fully substantiated by drawings, written statements or experimental data – although even in this case, extensive negotiation and clarification may be required before a mutually acceptable specification can be formulated[8].

Where a company does not operate this type of business, but instead is serving a large or mass market, then some kind of market research must supply the necessary information. In this case, the market research activity acts as the customer's 'agent' and its job is to ensure that the correct information is offered and incorporated in the specification. It is essential that this is drawn up jointly by the two parties – by the customer (or agent) and by the company – and that agreement is reached on all major project parameters before design work begins[9,10]. These parameters must include cost, time, performance and all other essential features.

Support for this approach comes from Mayall[11] who stresses that it is the responsibility of a professional designer to insist that a comprehensive specification is agreed at the beginning of a project. It may be argued that it is primarily the client's responsibility to provide adequate information at the start of a project but, in practice, the good designer will still satisfy himself that all relevant information has been extracted. In doing this, he will also wish to examine manufacturing programmes to determine production quantities, available processes, tooling restrictions, size limitations, etc.[12] Whilst this is particularly important when an external designer is being employed on a project, there are also many company-based designers who lack intimate knowledge of their company's production systems and for whom this stage is also highly important.

When preparing product specifications, companies may concentrate their efforts on acquiring information about users' requirements and in the process may overlook their own manufacturing capabilities. This deficiency arises generally because of a lack of production involvement at this stage. It seems to be a common view that the project conception is the sole responsibility of the design department and in practice nobody is likely to challenge the designers' 'rights' over the technical content of specific-ations[13]. However, it has been shown that considerable benefits can be gained by involving at this stage (and subsequently) not only production personnel but also specialists such as process planners, financial controllers and marketing staff[14]. Usually this results in substantial cost savings without loss of product quality or increase in project duration.

The dangers of embarking on design work without an adequate specification are illustrated by Lock[8]. He discusses how projects are likely to diversify from their original objectives under such circumstances. The result may be excessive design costs, high units costs and delayed product launch; he terms the phenomenon 'creeping improvement sickness' and identifies the quest for perfection as the basic problem. This point is taken further by Zarecor[15] who claims that designers and engineers are generally interested in exploiting technology and consequently tend to over-design. Hence, it is paramount that performance levels are specified before design starts and are adhered to when working towards a solution. He supports his argument by citing a case where a design team managed to double the performance of a product with only a 20% increase in costs. However, the added performance was simply not required by the market and nor would it accept an increased price.

These comments and examples are interesting, but they give little practical guidance about procedures for compiling a specification. For example, in addition to the participation of the designer and the customer (or representative) it seems largely a matter of circumstance as to who else is involved or excluded[16].

## 7.4 Specifications in Practice – Four Case Studies

This section reports on the approaches taken by four manufacturing companies to the task of preparing specifications for new products. These companies have been selected from those participating in the wider research project because they offer particularly clear insights into different aspects of the topic. In each case, a researcher has examined at first hand the procedures adopted and the decisions taken in attempting to arrive at a specification. The observations are presented in the form of four short case studies followed by a discussion.

## Company 1

This company manufactures gearboxes and employs about 200 people. It is large enough to have access to resources for investment in up-to-date shaft machining, gear cutting and case machining. However its senior managers consider it to be too small to sustain a range of standard gearboxes sufficiently wide to enable it to dictate to customers the product specifications most favourable to itself. The management recognises that in drawing up specifications it must be responsive to the requirements of customers, but at the same time it must attempt to standardise its production activities. Hence, a project moves through three phases before the product specification is determined:

- Contact with the customer to examine parameters and objectives.
- Initial outline design concept and budget costing based, as far as possible, on existing products.
- Meeting with customers to approve or modify proposal.

In general, a majority of enquiries arrive through the sales department where a questionnaire is used to extract the maximum amount of information from the customer. On this questionnaire are all the 'preferred' types of gearboxes and variations manufactured by the company. All items are coded and the sales representative ticks the appropriate features. Further information about special requirements is also included on the form. By this means, it is possible to evaluate the degree of 'novelty' involved in the project and thus, in the light of the quantities required, the desirability of the enquiry.

An example helps to clarify this company's approach. A customer requested a quotation for a multi-purpose gearbox. The initial contact was by telephone and this was followed by a rough sketch of requirements prepared by the customer. The designer re-worked this sketch into a form favourable to the company. At this stage the production engineer was consulted and his requirements were incorporated into the specification. Estimates of costs and times were prepared and transmitted to the customer

by the sales department. The customer responded with several modifications which were agreed and a firm order was placed. Detailed design commenced in accordance with the approved product specification. This company has a simple but comprehensive procedure for preparing specifications. Its operation reflects:
- Clearly defined objectives of the company, for example regarding standardisation, quantities, etc.
- A close working relationship between key personnel.
- An awareness of the need to give the customer the opportunity to influence the specification but not necessarily to dictate it.

## Company 2
Employing about 100 people, this company designs and manufactures material handling equipment. The product design process is initiated in one of two ways:
- The marketing department identifies an opportunity for a new product and constructs a broad outline of requirements; this is termed the 'commercial specification' which is then sent to the engineering department for a feasibility study.
- The engineering department reviews existing products to identify cases of excessive cost, inadequate performance, etc; this is followed by a feasibility study to establish the prospects for achieving improvements.

In both cases, a feasibility study is the mechanism by which a product specification is derived; the main purpose of the study is to determine whether a project is technically and economically sound. During the process of conducting the feasibility study, many formal and informal consultations take place. Requests for further information from the marketing department are common, and frequent approaches may be made to purchasing, costing and manufacturing. The study culminates with the presentation of several alternative design proposals together with the implications of each. This report is circulated widely in the company before a meeting of representatives of all departments agrees on the final product specification.

Any weakness in this procedure lies in the amount of time that may elapse between initiation and final agreement on a specification. The problem may be made worse when several different feasibility studies are being conducted simultaneously. Priorities tend to be decided by the engineering department, and do not necessarily reflect the true situation in the market place. A further danger is that the engineering department acts as a filter because it occupies the central role in the specification process. There is a tendency for practical considerations to be blocked, while excessive attention is devoted to technical issues. However, the company does have a record of successful product design and it would seem that the well established pattern of interdepartmental involvement acts as a satisfactory controlling influence.

## Company 3

With a workforce of about 220, this company manufactures ranges of standard and special architectural ironmongery such as doors, windows, handles, etc. As well as manufacturing products, it also provides a design and advisory service, mainly for commercial properties. The company does not have a single, standardised procedure for evaluating ideas and drawing up specifications although, in practice, two methods are found to predominate. The first applies to enquiries for special products received by the sales department. Observations show that up to 70% of these enquiries are declined by the sales personnel on the grounds of unsuitability. No formal guidelines exist – each decision is based on the judgement of the sales engineer and only rarely is reference made to any other section of the company. The remaining enquiries are passed to the design and estimating departments where quotations are prepared; following acceptance of a quotation by a customer, the design department finalises the product specification and commences design work. The second method operates when a specification is being devised for a new standard product. Analysis shows decisions are taken without reference to quantitative marketing or production data. Usually a project is initiated by the technical manager who derives his 'feel for the market' from participation in the activities of a trade association. The design team then prepares a number of alternative proposals, from which one is ultimately selected. The progress of a typical product specification is shown in *figure 7.2*.

The most striking feature about this company's approach to the preparation of the specification is the isolation of the design department. The department is responsible for providing almost all the information on which decisions are taken, yet it has little contact with the rest of the

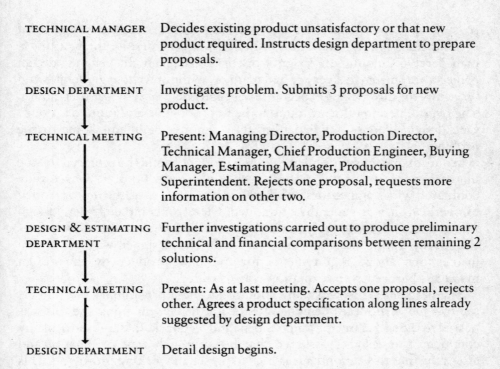

| | |
|---|---|
| TECHNICAL MANAGER | Decides existing product unsatisfactory or that new product required. Instructs design department to prepare proposals. |
| DESIGN DEPARTMENT | Investigates problem. Submits 3 proposals for new product. |
| TECHNICAL MEETING | Present: Managing Director, Production Director, Technical Manager, Chief Production Engineer, Buying Manager, Estimating Manager, Production Superintendent. Rejects one proposal, requests more information on other two. |
| DESIGN & ESTIMATING DEPARTMENT | Further investigations carried out to produce preliminary technical and financial comparisons between remaining 2 solutions. |
| TECHNICAL MEETING | Present: As at last meeting. Accepts one proposal, rejects other. Agrees a product specification along lines already suggested by design department. |
| DESIGN DEPARTMENT | Detail design begins. |

*Figure 7.2  Typical Specification Procedure for Standard Product – Company 3*

company or with customers. When specifications are being devised, the sales department is not represented at the technical meetings. Once initiated, design projects run smoothly but do not always yield results within the agreed time periods. It is significant that the production department frequently complains about unacceptable design features, despite the involvement it has at the technical meetings. This indicates a need for a direct input by production during the actual formulation of the specification.

## Company 4
Company 4 has about 600 employees involved in the manufacture of a range of food preparation machines. The firm is well established in markets in the United Kingdom and overseas and has manufacturing plants in

several other countries. There is no regular procedure for the compiling of specifications and the initiation of design projects, despite the fact that a considerable amount of design work is undertaken. In general, design projects are started in a very casual manner, without written guidelines and with only the most vague expectations, usually delivered by word of mouth. The overall design effort is found to be unproductive and morale is poor. One design exercise, studied from its inception, highlights some of the problems.

Senior management decided that one product should be replaced. It was unsatisfactory in several respects: the finish was poor, it was unsafe compared with competitors' machines, it was too costly, the motor tended to overheat, it was generally outmoded. Clearly a completely new design was required. Because everyone in the design department was already fully employed, a new designer was recruited. The designer was given oral instructions about requirements for the new product by the design manager. No written information was provided.

The designer set to work and soon produced a preliminary outline. He put together a model to demonstrate the line he was pursuing and this was passed to the sales director for comment and feedback. In the absence of any comment, the designer assumed that his approach was satisfactory and after a further three months was able to present a working prototype. This was rejected as completely unsatisfactory by the sales director.

Realising that he needed better information, the designer attempted to communicate directly with the sales director. This brought a rebuke from a senior manager in the design department who insisted that he should be involved in all communications. By now it was recognised that it would be in everyone's interest to have some kind of written specification. This was devised jointly by the manufacturing director, design manager, chief production engineer, sales director and the designer. A total of 9 months had now elapsed and a series of monthly meetings was started to monitor the project. Not until a meeting four months later was the specification finalised – perhaps significantly the sales director was absent. Thirteen months after the original start of the project, and after a great deal of misdirected effort, the project was ready to re-commence.

While this case study also indicates some problems of relationship and behaviour, the effect of an inadequate specification is clear. At no time was the designer entirely confident of what was required. He had no idea of the

|                                                                      | COMPANY 1                     | COMPANY 2                                                     | COMPANY 3                                        | COMPANY 4                                                  |
| -------------------------------------------------------------------- | ----------------------------- | ------------------------------------------------------------ | ------------------------------------------------ | --------------------------------------------------------- |
| Primary responsibility for compiling specifications                  | Sales, design, production     | Engineering (incl. design)                                   | Design                                           | Design, production                                        |
| Design contribution                                                  | **                            | **                                                           | **                                               | *                                                         |
| Production contribution                                              | **                            | **                                                           | o                                                | o                                                         |
| Financial contribution                                               | **                            | *                                                            | *                                                | o                                                         |
| Marketing contribution                                               | **                            | *                                                            | o                                                | o                                                         |
| Comprehensiveness of specification                                   | Adequate Information          | Imbalance in favour of technical aspects                     | Generally inadequate information                 | Inadequate or misleading information                      |
| Effectiveness of specification as guidelines for design project      | Satisfactory                  | Satisfactory but supplementary information required          | Unsatisfactory – too many aspects unspecified    | Unreliable compiled without commitment or conviction      |
| Subsequent progress of product design                                | Good                          | Good                                                         | Variable                                         | Poor                                                      |

*Key:* ** is a substantial contribution which significantly influences the final outcome.
   * is a casual contribution which does not significantly influence the final outcome.
   o is where there is no contribution.

*Table 7.1 Summary of Analysis of Specifications*

design priorities nor of the cost and time constraints. His only information came from observation of the original product that he was attempting to replace and the comments of the design manager.

## 7.5 Discussion

These four companies demonstrate a range of approaches to the task of drawing up a design specification. The main features of each company's approach is summarised in *table 7.1*.

*Company 1* shows how a balanced approach to the specification is likely to lead to good design performance. Starting with a clear statement of the requirements of the customer, analysed with the aid of a questionnaire/checklist, this company then proceeded to identify all the key components of the specification. All departments participated in the drafting of the specification, which was prepared against a clear statement of the design objectives of the company. This may be contrasted with the extreme case of *Company 4* where no recognisable specification existed, at least during the first 13 months that the design project was investigated. Without the guidance of a specification, the relationship between design and production functions was highly unsatisfactory; the relationship between design and sales even more so. Between these two approaches, lie those of the other companies in this study. They help to demonstrate the way that the various strengths and weaknesses of the specification may be reflected in the ensuing design performance. For example, *Company 3* shows that a low input from production coupled with a strong design contribution may lead to considerable friction between designers and production specialists.

In relation to the literature discussed earlier, a number of points may be made. The most important of these concerns the nature of the total design process and the role of the specification within it. It will be recalled that much of the literature tends to perceive the design process as a series of distinct steps. These four companies clearly show the dangers of such a view. The designer in *Company 4* followed a concept of moving from step to step – from problem to sketch to model to prototype. The importance of feedback of information was minimised to such an extent that the project eventually stagnated and had to be re-started (in other circumstances it

might well have been abandoned). The absence of a competent specification excluded the possibility of any encouragement to the designer to
develop an 'interactive approach'. Similarly, the design team in *Company
3* prepared a specification by progressing steadily from one point to the
next, effectively preventing the input of modifications by always offering
the alternatives from which the choice had to be made (see *figure 7.2*). The
design activities of *Companies 1 and 2* more closely resemble the
diagrammatic concept outlined in *figure 7.1* Not only was the customer
considered central to the whole design process but the importance of
interaction between departments was emphasised, including during the
period while the specification was being prepared. *Figure 7.1* serves as a
reminder of the need to 'balance' the component parts of the design
activity, and this small sample of companies indicates the dangers of
losing this balance.

Turning to the literature most directly concerned with drawing up a
specification, it can be seen that the views of Mayall[11] are generally
supported. In particular, the case studies confirm the need to agree
specifications before design begins and to ensure that all major parameters
are specified. Lock's concern about irrelevance and diversification caused
by substandard specifications[8] cannot be tested against the evidence
available so far from this research project although the performance of
several of the companies suggests that his theory of 'creeping improvement sickness' might well be correct. The views expressed by Scott-
Wilson[13] are largely confirmed by the cases reported here: it is still a
widespread belief that the technical contents of specifications are the
exclusive responsibility of designers. Thus, the approach suggested by
Dangerfield[14] would seem to offer wide scope for improved performance
and the advice offered by Betts[16] perhaps points in the right direction: it
pays to look closely at not only who is involved, but more important still
who is excluded. From these case examinations, it is difficult to predict
any relationship between the format of the specification (i.e. whether
verbal or written guidelines) and its effect on the final outcome of the
product design. Information from interviews in a large number of
companies does show that a majority of firms prepare some kind of
written specification, but it is evident from these direct observations that it
is the quality and scope of the specification that is more likely to be the
significant factor rather than the form of presentation.

## 7.6 Conclusions

On the basis of the work reported in this chapter, a number of guidelines relating to product specifications are proposed. Although design is not a mechanistic activity, and it would be unrealistic to attempt to provide universal rules, the following generalisations will be valid in many cases.
  - Design projects should proceed against a written specification.
  - The authorship of the specification is not important providing that all functions within the company have the opportunity to input data.
  - The central role of the customer must be acknowledged and preserved.
  - A balance of conflicting requirements must be achieved and agreed by all functions.
  - Deadlines, budgets and reporting systems must be defined and agreed.
  - Where possible the specification should be finalised before design work begins.

This research indicates that considerable scope exists in industry for the improvement of the specification drafting process. Research on a wider scale is necessary in order to quantify the extent of the problem and to propose more comprehensive guidelines to assist designers and their colleagues.

# 8 Case Study: Alpha Vending – Product Design in Small Firms

## 8.1 Introduction

Up to now, this book has been concerned mainly with the problems of managing product design in large companies. To some extent, this is a reflection of the fact that in recent years considerable attention has been given to the development of new products in large firms. Several important studies have provided valuable assessments of the factors which influence the product design process, but very little work has been done with small companies. In some cases it was intentional that the research should concentrate on large companies, but in others there is evidence that larger firms were more willing to co-operate than smaller ones and that this, rather than any research decision, dictated the form of the investigation.

In view of the contribution made to national prosperity by small companies, it is a pity that more work has not been done to examine their problems and practices. In the United Kingdom, small businesses (taken to be those employing less than 200 people) play a crucial part in the economic life of the country, providing over a quarter of the total employment and about 20 per cent of the Gross National Product.[1] Furthermore, it is from these small companies that the next generation of large businesses will develop so future prosperity depends directly upon their present success.

Despite this, the body of knowledge relating specifically to the management of small businesses forms a minute part of the published management literature. It has been said that small firms are so imperfectly understood that no adequate 'general theory' has yet been proposed[2] to explain their operation either individually or taken together as a component of the national economy. As part of the research work discussed in chapter 7, an investigation is taking place into the problems faced by small firms which engage in product design. After looking at some published material relevant to the topic, this chapter goes on to present a detailed examination of one small firm which is taking part in the research project.

## 8.2 Product Design and Small Firms

Just as in large companies, design in small companies will usually be found as part of a wider 'innovation' process. In relation to products, this process embraces all the activities involved in progressing from initial idea to eventual realisation of commercial success. It may entail many areas of expertise such as marketing, finance and production, as well as design[3]. The degree of homogeneity existing between design and other functions within the innovation process has been found to vary according to factors like frequency of new product introduction and general complexity or predictability of operations[4], but in general, there is strong support for the view that close integration of component activities is an important prerequisite for successful innovation[5].

It has been reported[6] that as few as 20 per cent of new products actually launched into the market become commercial successes. Another study[7] puts the figure at 33 per cent but also shows that for each ultimately successful product an average of 58 ideas will have been discarded, some at a very early stage but others only after the investment of much time and effort. While certain prominent companies consistently out-perform these statistics many others enjoy little success and attempting to design new products is clearly an awesome task for them. Yet the penalty for not manufacturing up-to-date products can be even more severe; unsatisfactory product performance is a major cause of company failure especially amongst smaller companies.

The reasons behind the high rate of failure have been explored by a number of researchers; Gold[8] suggests that many firms wrongly estimate the anticipated technological benefits of innovation when framing product plans. In particular the time required to achieve effective performance of an innovation is often under-estimated while the anticipated adoption rate is over-estimated. In small firms these weaknesses might be accounted for by shortages of the experienced personnel needed to conduct project appraisals. Some researchers argue that this weakness is more than offset by the entrepreneurial drive, single mindedness, ability to act, and enthusiasm[9] of small companies, but this seems highly debatable. As Rothwell[10] points out, on the basis of his comparative studies, successful innovators outperform failures in all areas of competence. In particular, his work indicates the importance of combining a thorough understanding of users' needs with sound design skills (including being receptive to outside technology) and authoritative project leadership.

The methodology adopted by Rothwell and his colleagues featured the examination of pairs of similar projects, each pair containing one successful and one relatively unsuccessful project. Although the researchers took steps to eliminate biased results, it must be a criticism of this work that the selection of the pairings itself cannot be ruled out as a determinant of the findings. The work of Langrish et al.[11] retrospectively investigated innovations which had been granted Queen's Awards for technological innovation. A central feature of this research was the examination of statements and publicity material prepared by each of the firms in the study. Perhaps not surprisingly, the results of this research stressed success factors such as 'the presence of an outstanding person' and 'help from government sources'. These are the kinds of points that might have been given undeserved prominence by firms at the time they were trying to impress a panel of assessors, and then became embodied in the folklore of the companies. However, this study is useful because it highlights the problems experienced by some companies, particularly smaller ones, with respect to shortages of resources and lack of access to sufficiently developed technology, both of which were seen as factors detracting from the progress of innovation.

A more recent survey has been reported by Topalian[12] in which a total of 510 respondents (described as 'managers, clients and designers') were asked to indicate agreement or disagreement with 28 statements on difficulties perceived in the management of design projects. These statements had been 'distilled from those typically raised by managers and designers', and the survey was conducted in the United Kingdom and North America. The most common reasons cited to explain why design projects can be difficult to manage included:

- To manage them effectively requires getting involved in a wider field than indicated by the problem as originally stated.

- Frequently the designer has to educate the client (or senior manager) in design management, as well as get on with the project.
- Senior managers rarely appreciate what design projects involve.

Topalian acknowledges his relatively small sample size but argues that analysis of a number of sub-samples reveals consistency in response profiles. This may be the case, but there are still weaknesses in this study which tend to undermine the usefulness of the results. Firstly, no reference is made to other work relevant to the topic, indeed it is clearly assumed that no other data is available. Secondly, the statistical treatment of results seems arbitrary and insufficiently rigorous. Despite these reservations, the survey does reinforce the view that both managers and designers believe that most difficulties arise through managerial rather than technical problems.

In a report on a major research project into industrial innovation, Parker[13] identifies the important advantages of large companies over small ones: their ability to develop and use sophisticated technology. As far as small companies are concerned, he deduces that they:

- Tend to be over optimistic in tackling new products.
- Are prone to under–rate the likely emergence of competition.
- Are often content to market single products in narrow market sectors.
- Lag in updating their manufacturing processes.

He also reports that several small firms in his study felt the need of a 'broker' for technical information, indicating weaknesses in both the managerial and technical resources available. Whilst these comments are interesting and may well be substantially accurate, there is insufficient detail in the report to allow confirmation of this. Studies by other researchers are dismissed by Parker as being of 'little practical value' and apparently no attempt has been made to integrate other work into the project.

A more recent publication[14] deriving from the project presents certain 'guidelines' for innovation but it is difficult to see what new data has been derived for the material resembles much other innovation literature with little indication of any major input from the research project. It is also noticeable that the guidelines are presented with only large companies in mind (hence reference to 'group headquarters' and 'subsidiary companies' etc.).

Even companies whose managers are aware of the factors which influence the design process may fail to achieve their intended objectives. A common problem is the inability, or unwillingness, of managers to anticipate the compromises which inevitably occur during a design project. The idea that 'at each stage of development a product looks better than it ever will again' has been described as the first law of product planning[15] and neatly describes the short-sighted optimism which often surrounds new projects. Judgements about the adequacy of technical capability, for example, are often quite unrealistic because of a lack of understanding of the normal demands of the organisation, in addition to those generated by the new project. Sometimes misplaced optimism for new ideas may lead firms down paths which are inappropriate, particularly with regard to general market conditions. Harper[16] argues that diversity, luxury and variety are appropriate when customers incomes are rising but in times of economic depression, attention ought to be concentrated on basic products and high profit products, with imaginative use of existing technology rather than speculative new technology.

Technical aspects of product design may be especially troublesome to small firms; the interface between design and production is an important example. In larger firms where both design engineering and production engineering are strongly represented, there are likely to be few problems in designing components that are functional, reliable and easy to manufacture. This may not be the case in situations with low staff numbers where designers must themselves select manufacturing processes (involving knowledge of relationships between material properties and fabricability, cost of materials, operating variables, etc.) as well as attend to the 'traditional' design aspects such as stress analysis, kinetics, friction and wear, etc. These problems may be exacerbated in small firms because of lack of access to reference data for comparison with suppliers' data which, according to Datsko[17], is often misleading and inaccurate.

## 8.3 Some Conclusions from the Literature

In general, the literature indicates that small firms have to face many of the same problems associated with product design in large companies, but the emphasis may be different. Lack of expertise and generally limited resources may be the major constraints affecting small companies[18], in contrast to the resistance to change and organisational inflexibility that often characterise bigger firms.

To achieve success in product design, all companies large or small must attain appropriate levels of performance in certain vital functions. The nature of the functions will vary between projects but will typically include:
- Management functions in such areas as marketing finance, project management, etc.
- Technical functions such as design, mechanical engineering, electronics, material science, etc.

In large companies, the availability of personnel with the necessary skills is not likely to be a problem and, if there are shortages of skills, resources will generally be available to recruit or transfer staff. The specialist skills demanded in product design are usually different from those required for routine workflow operations and as shown by Child[19] there is a linear relationship between total non-workflow employment (in activities such as purchasing, design and finance) and total organisational employment. In other words, the larger the company the greater the chance that all necessary specialist skills will be present.

A further example of this relationship between availability of skills and firm size comes in a study[20] concerned with the adoption of new materials. This found that material specialists could be identified only in very large companies; in small companies, decisions about materials were made by groups of non-specialists, often with little up-to-date awareness of material developments. This suggests that when tackling the design of new products, small firms may experience difficulty in assembling sufficient skills from within their own boundaries. In such cases, one or both of the following strategies may be adopted:
- Limiting projects to those requiring only skills readily available or easily learnt by existing staff. This approach may involve considerable risk because the range of new product ideas will be restricted and because the dominance of the specialist skills which happen to be available may well lead to faulty decisions. For example lack of knowledge of new materials, which may potentially be highly suitable for a particular application, is likely to occur where there is little awareness of current outside developments. Failure of a new project may then follow as a direct result.

- Selecting projects against the criterion of general appropriateness without overriding consideration being given to skills limitations. Ideally, selection of projects will be preceded by a systematic analysis of the company and its environment. After the choice of the project, new skills must then be secured as necessary to facilitate the innovation process.

There are numerous ways in which small companies can obtain access to extra skills, although, as Moody shows in his discussion on the use of industrial designers, there may be disagreement amongst in-company specialists over the introduction of outside skills[21]. In such situations, the role of top management becomes crucial since it alone can decide the real needs of the project.

*Table 8.1* represents an attempt to list some of the ways in which small companies can acquire extra skills together with the possible limitations in each case. The ultimate limitation will always depend on the energy and determination of the top management since, as the table indicates, most skills can be obtained from a variety of sources.

## 8.4 Case Study of a Small Firm

This case study reports actual events although all names have been changed. Alpha Vending Ltd. operates from a 1000 m² factory in central England. The firm started business around 1930 and was controlled by the founder until the late 1960s when the present MD (managing director) acquired the majority shareholding. The MD previously worked as the marketing manager for a major confectionery company and has extensive knowledge of the commercial aspects of the vending industry. His skills as a salesman have ensured a steady supply of orders for Alpha in a market segment which has attracted powerful competititors. The company employs about 20 people and, as shown in *figure 8.1* most of these are involved in manufacturing operations.

For many years, Alpha has concentrated on the manufacture of small, wall-mounted vending machines which dispense chocolate bars and similar packaged products. These machines consist of a coin-accepting mechanism, and a product dispensing mechanism, housed in a pressed steel casing. The

| Examples of skills required: | Possible sources of extra skills (limitations); |
|---|---|
| **Finance**<br>— fund raising<br>— project evaluation<br>— financial management | Consultants (cost, availability, selection problems)<br>Financial institutions (willingness to help, ability to understand problems). Small firms advisory services (limited resources).<br>Funding bodies eg NRDC, ICFC (may not be interested in small projects, may be unwilling to bear risk). |
| **Marketing**<br>— market research<br>— data analysis | Consultants (cost, availability, selection problems)<br>Agencies (cost, availability)<br>Business Schools (speed of response, availability of staff/students) |
| **Design**<br>— specialist technical<br>— drafting/testing<br>— general design<br>— legal aspects | Consultants (cost, availability, selection problems)<br>Temporary/casual employees (cost, quality, availability, control)<br>Research/trade associations (membership requirements, fees, confidentiality)<br>Universities/colleges etc (availability, coincidence of interest)<br>Design Council and similar bodies (membership requirement, appropriateness of skills) |
| **Production**<br>— production engineering<br>— project management | Subcontractors (control, quality, cost)<br>Consultants (cost, availability, selection problems)<br>Joint venture with other firm(s) (suitability, compromises involved, confidentiality, interpersonal relations) |

*Table 8.1 Sources of Extra Skills Available to Small Firms Designing New Products and Possible Limitations*

coin mechanisms are bought as sub-assemblies from a specialist manu-facturer. Most of the other components are made in-house and are mild steel pressings. Hence, the factory is mainly concerned with presswork and assembly operations. This is reflected in the plant and equipment: guillotines, presses, stud and spot welding machines, together with ancillary equipment such as grinders, drilling machines and electric saws. There is also a small paint spraying facility.

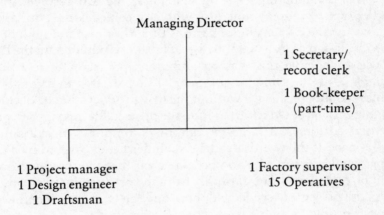

Managing Director

1 Secretary/
record clerk

1 Book-keeper
(part-time)

1 Project manager
1 Design engineer
1 Draftsman

1 Factory supervisor
15 Operatives

*Figure 8.1  Organisation of Alpha Vending Limited*

Much of the plant is old and inefficient, a consequence of the lack of attention given to the factory and its operations. The MD has always been preoccupied with the commercial side of Alpha and has little knowledge of, or interest in, production matters. He relies upon long-serving and experienced employees to manage the factory on a day-to-day basis. Unfortunately, no clear technical leadership has emerged and inefficient work practices, poor working conditions, low wages and low productivity are all in evidence. Nevertheless, Alpha has continued to 'tick over' and has managed to preserve a reputation for good quality products.

During the last few years, frequent changes in the prices of dispensed products have caused serious problems in the vending industry. With each price rise, coin mechanisms must be rebuilt or replaced to accommodate the new coin configuration. The MD decided that the solution to this problem lay in the design of a new generation of vending machines, which unlike their predecessors, would not be totally mechanical but would incorporate electronic controls. These machines would be capable of instant adjustment to suit any price of product and, with further development, could offer other facilities such as change–giving, or even some form of electronic interaction with the customer.

As well as updating existing machines, the MD resolved to develop another type of vending unit, also with electronic features, to satisfy a new demand for the dispensing of cartons of soft drinks and milk derivatives. Thus the design of two major new products was initiated. In the light of the resources available this was an ambitious programme; few funds were available from within the company. The MD felt so strongly that his business could not survive without the new products that he decided to risk building up a large overdraft to fund the project. He managed to persuade a potential customer, a large international company, to guarantee a substantial part of the overdraft, the remainder being covered by a charge on his personal property. It soon became clear that the rapidly growing debt could be repaid only out of profits from the new products. In other words, unless the project succeeded, Alpha would be bankrupt. There were other resource problems which had to be overcome:

## Design team

No formal design and development section existed in Alpha. Indeed, no drawings or records were available of existing products and any modifications requested by a customer were carried out in the factory usually by one particularly highly experienced employee, Colin. This employee had worked for Alpha for nearly 30 years and carried in his head most of the company's technical information. Sometimes he used this information as a bargaining counter when in dispute with the MD who was well aware that without Colin's presence and cooperation the factory would be unable to function. Colin agreed to transfer from general production work and spend most of his time on the design of the two new machines. He was joined by Dave who had been with Alpha for 3 or 4 years. Dave had been recruited as a production engineer but had been encouraged to dabble in design projects. He had a degree in mechanical engineering and had worked for several other firms before joining Alpha. He was appointed Project

Manager and Colin was designated Design Engineer. They worked alone for some months before they were joined by Peter, a draftsman who had come to work at Alpha on a temporary basis as part of a sandwich degree course which he was following as a mature student.

## Technical skills

Between them, the members of the design team had many of the skills necessary to tackle the project. Dave was a good 'ideas man' and was able to propose novel concepts and solutions. Colin was skilled in techniques of sheet metal work and was particularly good at adapting existing conventional solutions to satisfy new problems. However, both men were so strongly influenced by the designs of existing products that this inhibited their work. Peter was a competent design draftsman (although this skill was little regarded by the others who disliked the discipline that accurate drawings implied) and he also contributed many useful design ideas, when allowed to do so.

Some vital skills were missing. In particular, no one in Alpha had any experience in electronics, which was to be the basis of operation of new machines. The MD decided to approach the electronic engineering department of a local university. This department agreed to collaborate and a member of its research staff, an experienced circuit designer, was assigned to the project. The work was to be funded entirely by Alpha but, since a microprocessor control unit was the ultimate aim, the MD expected to receive a grant from a government fund set up to promote the development of microelectronics.

## Procurement and purchasing skills

These skills were in short supply. For normal production, only a relatively small range of items was required: sheet steel, fasteners, coin mechanisms, etc. These were obtained routinely from local suppliers and unfamiliar purchases were a rare occurrence. As the project gathered pace, increasingly large quantities of unfamiliar items had to be procured. This work had to be done by the design team and it became obvious that many over-expensive and otherwise inappropriate decisions had been made because of lack of time and experience. Towards the climax of the project, as supplies for final prototypes were being secured, a number of particularly expensive mistakes were made.

## Workshop facilities

An area of the factory was cleared and partitioned off to form a crude workshop. A few benches and shelves were found and some basic equipment provided. The area was barely satisfactory: the noise of the factory intruded and space was inadequate. As prototypes were built they had to be moved out to allow adequate access to them. Constant use had to be made of normal factory machines such as power presses and spot welders. Inevitably this caused many problems of disruption, both to production of regular output and to the design project. The proximity of the workshops to the factory gave rise to frequent calls upon the team to attend to routine manufacturing problems and the project was sometimes neglected for long periods as a consequence.

## Planning and control

The deficiencies of the company in planning and control became painfully evident. At no stage did anyone prepare any formal written specification for either of the two new machines, nor was there any kind of design brief. In discussions, the MD would convey an idea of what was required together with any specific comments from prospective customers. Few written records were kept so dimensions, capacities, performance, appearance, etc. all changed constantly as new ideas were tried out. When eventually completed, the final prototypes of one of the machines were judged by the customers to have unacceptable defects, such as excessive dimensions, which had been specified previously and should not have caused problems.

With no experience of this scale of project, the MD's estimates of the duration of the work were highly inaccurate and always over-optimistic. He gave assurances of completion dates to prospective customers and, as these slipped, he compounded his problems by offering promises of extra features in return for extra time. After it had been running for over a year, the project was set for disaster. Alpha was heavily in debt, customers and backers were losing interest, and the design team had lost most of its enthusiasm. As a last resort, the MD hired an executive experienced in the running of design projects. The executive made an assessment of what could be realistically achieved within the final deadlines offered by the customers. He insisted that the designs were to be frozen and any extra features postponed until the basic prototypes had been accepted and approved by the customers. It was apparent to him that the design team, in the absence of any effective leadership, was now treating the project as a hobby and felt no sense of urgency or prospect of success.

In order to achieve the manufacture of the prototypes, the executive placed some of the work with a specialist sub-contractor; a course of action which was initially rejected with a threat of a strike but was grudgingly accepted when the seriousness of the predicament was explained. He also split up the design team to reinforce a sense of urgency and sent one member 'on secondment' to the sub-contractor in order to coordinate the work. As a result of these actions, prototype machines of an agreed specification were delivered within the deadline. The main prospective customer spent several weeks testing the machine before deciding not to place an order or offer further support.

## 8.5 Discussion

Several important issues emerge from this case history. Probably the most striking is the way that the project, set up to design and manufacture a new product, rapidly began to dominate normal activities to such an extent that the survival of the company was put at risk. The basic problem was one of inadequate management; the project lacked competent and experienced leadership. From the beginning, no serious attempt was made to anticipate the resource demands of the project, nor to forecast the effects on existing operations. In this respect the findings of other researchers are supported: design projects become difficult to manage because of the unexpectedly wide range of problems which they generate. In this case these problems included:

- Lack of creativity and flexibility within the design team caused by over-familiarity with existing practice and products.
- New skills demanded by the project such as purchasing, record keeping and electronic expertise, none of which could be supplied from within the firm.
- Inadequate financial resources resulting in prolonged negotiations with outside backers and creditors.
- The need to identify, pursue and engage sources of technical assistance outside the firm.

These and other problems grew to assume great significance because certain basic instruments of management were absent. Notable was the lack of any kind of design brief or specification, other than the most basic (unwritten) indications of requirements. This serious failing of management was directly responsible for much wasted effort on technical problems which could have been circumvented had the implications of the project been correctly analysed during the preparation of a design brief. A brief would also have shown that the technical facilities within the company were inadequate for the proposed scale of project and would certainly have exposed the dangers of attempting to manage two new designs simultaneously.

The 'entrepreneurial drive' which, as noted earlier, is often associated with small businesses was strongly evident in this case. The commitment to the project was undeniably firm, probably disadvantageously so, since much of the optimism generated would not have been justified by any disinterested analysis. The technical and financial limitations of the company suggest that incremental developments of existing products and technology, guided by appropriate marketing information, would have yielded much better results than the unfamiliar electronic technology which was selected.

This illustrates the extent to which outside skills may be used by firms. The use of electronic specialists from a university department worked well, although lack of knowledge of electronics in the firm caused considerable unease and speculation about the quality of the work. The same problems were experienced in respect of other 'sub-contracted' technical work and this underlines the need for a technically competent coordinator in situations where a project extends beyond the normal boundaries of the firm. In this case, no such person was involved in the project until a late stage.

The firm was unable to obtain extra skills in purchasing and approached several consultants before finding one able to administer the financial needs of the project. Exhaustive use was made of government and official agencies in attempts to locate additional skills, but with only limited success. Part of the problem was that neither the agencies nor the firm fully understood the implications of the project. This leads to the conclusion that there is a need for certain minimum levels of technical and management skills within a firm before successful use can be made of additional outside skills. One implication of this is that a realistic level of finance must be available to underwrite basic needs; if this level (which can only be determined by evaluation of each case) cannot be provided, successful product innovation is unlikely to be achieved.

## 8.6 Conclusions

This case study of a small company illustrates a number of issues relating to product design already noted by other researchers and management writers. The main weaknesses preventing success in this case were:
- Over ambitious scale of project in relation to the size of the firm and its resources.
- Inadequate design management and leadership skills.

Within the latter category, three aspects in particular seemed to have a marked influence on the progress of the project:

**Design brief**
No formal, agreed brief existed to give the design team guidance or to allow the company to measure progress towards targets. It may be that small firms find such documents especially difficult to compile or do not consider them necessary for their scale of operation.

**Use of outside skills**
Because appropriate skills were not available in this firm, a large part of the design work had to be sub-contracted. This undermined control, co-ordination and relevance; maintaining a satisfactory balance between in-house and outside work is an important consideration for small firms.

**Interface between design and production**
In this small firm, general scarcity of technical resources dictated that production equipment had to be used extensively for design work. This gave rise to considerable disruption and conflict which, in turn, harmed the relationship between production and design personnel to the extent that vital information did not flow freely. It is probable that this problem has to be faced and resolved by most small firms when engaged in product design work.

# 9 Product Improvement and Value Analysis

## 9.1 Introduction

So far attention has been concentrated upon design work in relation to new products, but of course in most companies effort needs to be directed to existing products as well. Sooner or later, all firms operating in competitive markets will find that their products are less profitable than they used to be. This is because other manufacturers will have introduced alternative products which are cheaper to buy or more attractive to use (or both).

Unfortunately, many companies believe that design stops at the launch of a new product and are unprepared when sales eventually start to decline. Their response may be limited to an inadequate 'face-lift' or, even worse, resignation to the fate of having to abandon the particular market altogether. In most cases, such responses would be unnecessary if a 're-design policy' had been worked out and implemented. The completion of the original design project should be seen as just the start of a permanent design programme which will ensure that the product remains up-to-date and successful. Such a programme should include ways of monitoring product performance and changes in the market place. Also needed is some means of evaluating the appropriateness of the design of the product as circumstances alter and in the light of changes made to competitors' products.

There are several ways of tackling this work. One is to hand over the job to the design department, although this may have drawbacks. Another way is to retain a design consultant to keep a 'watching brief' and to advise on a regular basis about product strategy. The dilemma in this approach is that the best design consultant for this kind of work would be one who is highly active in the field; but such activity may well be achieved only if the consultant is also working for other firms. This may restrict the range and depth of advice which can be provided since the consultant will be careful not to disclose confidential information.

Whilst for most firms it is the discipline of reviewing products that is important, rather than who is involved in doing it, the most effective way is often to use small groups of employees drawn from different parts of the company to evaluate products and designs. For some time this approach has been increasingly used with success to tackle manufacturing problems – readers will be familiar with the term 'Quality Circle' often used to describe this group activity. There is no reason why 'Design Circles' should not operate in the same manner and, in fact, they have been for many years, but they are usually called value analysis groups.

## 9.2 Programmes for Product Re-design

To ensure long-term prosperity, all companies should adopt some means of critically reviewing their products. Rather than waiting for disaster to strike, the object of the review should be to identify at an early stage those products which are beginning to lose their attractiveness to customers. As just indicated, the mechanism of this review can vary a great deal. In some companies the marketing department may operate a continuous review of product performance; in others an occasional review might be thought adequate. Wherever it is decided that the primary responsibility should lie, the following points need to be observed:

**Priority assessment**
Very few companies manufacture only a single product, so most firms need to identify which products are most valuable to them. Points like annual sales value and contribution to overheads are clear indicators, but so are brand image and the extent to which a product fills a gap in the market. It may be more difficult to decide about design features – what are the current trends in terms of styling, colour, presentation etc.? How do the company's products compare with those of competitors from a design point of view? Which products are judged by customers to be offering good value for money and which are less well-regarded?

## Basis of review

Ideally this should be on a continuous basis with information constantly updated, not only for the product under review but also for its competitors. Top management should expect to see regular summaries of product performance in just the same way that it expects to be kept informed about financial performance. It may even be possible to devise methods for describing 'product health' or 'design quality' in terms of indices or ratios, so that the position relative to other companies may be seen clearly.

## 'Trigger points'

Each firm must define the point in the review programme at which a re-design exercise should be initiated. Depending on the type of product, it may be on the basis of a single indicator such as a fall in design competitiveness caused by new products from other firms, falling market share or a combination of different factors. A very good case can be made in support of a policy of holding regular re-design exercises, as well as maintaining the 'watching brief' to detect falling competitiveness. The rate of progress in most branches of technology is sufficiently fast that few designs more than two or three years old cannot be improved, usually in ways that achieve both savings in production costs and better matching of product features to customers' needs. Consequently most firms should think in terms of a two-edged approach:

– *Product reviews* on a continuous basis to give advanced warning of loss of competitive advantage and to initiate re-design exercises as soon as they become necessary.

– *Regular re-design exercises* to enable advantage to be taken of latest technology and thus to maintain profitability at the highest possible levels.

Often, the most obvious way to re-design a product will seem to be to hand it over to the design department, perhaps to the individual or team which did the original work. When it looks as though fairly drastic changes might be required this may be the only realistic course. However, there are serious drawbacks to this practice. For a start, the fact that the existing design is familar to the design department, and is probably viewed with some pride, might severely diminish the prospects of any really inspired changes. Also, even where the design department does have good working relationships with the rest of the company, it may be very difficult for it to evaluate the implications of change proposals.

To overcome these problems, some kind of collaborative re-design exercise is recommended. Unlike the process of designing a new product, where complex specifications have to be skilfully converted into design solutions, the problem in a re-design exercise is usually the less complicated one of modifying the existing solutions to achieve useful improvements. Thus, designers might be joined by representatives from other departments to tackle the project on a team basis. Where these representatives are truly involved in the exercise, rather than being regarded simply as 'advisors' to the design specialists, quite exciting results may be obtained. 'Value Analysis' is a set of techniques based on such a multi-disciplinary team approach.

## 9.3 Value Analysis

As a technique for improving design standards, reducing costs and boosting profitability, value analysis is badly under-exploited. Although it was just after World War II that the method was first developed and shown to be effective, few companies in the United Kingdom use it regularly today. Perhaps this is because the ideas behind value analysis (VA) are so logical and straightforward that managers feel the technique is being applied as a matter of course in their companies. They can point to a description of VA such as 'the elimination, by critical analysis of design, of unnecessary product cost while retaining or improving value to the customer', and comment that this is what they are trying to do all the time, so that no special approach is needed.

It is a pity that VA is dismissed in this way. The main feature of VA is that it is an organised and deliberate procedure, which should not be confined to products in trouble, but should be applied to currently successful products as well. By having regular, systematic reviews of product designs, maximum advantage can be taken of new materials, techniques and methods as they become available. But more than this, since value analysis should always be a team exercise using representatives from different parts of the company (e.g. production, sales, accounting, etc.), features valued by the customer can be identified, preserved and improved in a way that may not happen if technical specialists are used alone. Value analysis is so called

because it focuses upon the 'values' offered by the product to customers. It works by concentrating on the reduction of the direct manufacturing cost of the product while preserving, or improving, these values – basically the technical, artistic, ergonomic and economic features described in chapter 6. In essence, VA operates by:
 – Identifying value features or specific functions of the product.
 – Examining alternative ways of achieving these.
 – Choosing the way that entails least cost coupled with maximum satisfaction for the customer.

VA may change the design of the product and also, where appropriate, the method of manufacture. Every component of the current product is examined in turn, so the maximum possible cost savings and value improvements can be achieved. Value analysis techniques have been well reported and there are numerous references which may be consulted for details of methodologies and case histories.[1-4] Some experts describe procedures involving twelve or more steps, but for most applications a much simpler approach is satisfactory.

### Stage 1 – Familiarisation
Some team members will be more familiar than others with the various components of the product under investigation, but all need to see drawings, specifications, cost breakdowns, unassembled examples of the product, etc. Immediately the benefit of the multi-functional team will be apparent: the accountant explaining the significance of the cost figures, the production engineer detailing the manufacturing stages involved. The first step must be to find out as accurately as possible the present costs and values associated with the product. Cost elements for each component should be broken down into labour costs and material costs, and should be recorded for reference during subsequent stages of the exercise. Value elements may be more difficult to identify and this is where the benefit of the team approach will become clear. The marketing representative should be able to give an informed opinion about the values which the customer seeks in the products and its competitors. But frequently this opinion is challenged, alternative assessments considered, and a consensus achieved. In the next section a method for evaluating design is discussed which may be used at this stage of a VA exercise. Again this result should be noted for reference at later stages. Finally it is interesting to record the manufacturing times

applicable to the existing design so that improvements in productivity can be calculated at the end of the exercise.

## Stage 2 – Speculation
This is the most crucial part of a Value Analysis exercise. Taking each component in turn, the team subjects it to critical examination. The first question is always 'Can we eliminate it?' Surprisingly often the answer is 'Yes'. It may be necessary to alter an adjacent part to ensure that the function is not lost, but usually there will still be an immediate cost saving. If the component is essential and cannot be eliminated, then the team must try to find other cost savings by making some change to it. Free-ranging 'brainstorming' techniques may be used by the team to produce ideas for change, although without an experienced team leader, inhibitions may prevent the realisation of full potential. In most exercises, the best results are obtained by starting with a 'structured' approach; a checklist of appropriate questions that will give the team a basis for generating ideas. For example: 'Can we use a standard part?' 'Can we use a cheaper material?' 'Can we use less material?' and so on. After the checklist has been used to highlight the most promising improvements that may be possible, the team is then likely to follow the leads provided with a high expectation of success and a corresponding lack of inhibition.

## Stage 3 – Examination
After each component has been analysed in turn, the team will find that there are a small number of changes which can be made to improve or maintain the product as far as the customer is concerned, and to bring cost benefits to the company. The effect of each alteration must be examined and the total effect of all changes in combination should be determined. Only if the team is certain that the product remains at least as good as it was originally, can it recommend that the changes should be implemented. Often there will be several courses of action available; a decision may have to be taken whether to recommend maximum design improvement, maximum cost saving or a balance of each.

## Stage 4 – Implementation
The team should complete its analysis by calculating the extent of the overall cost–saving which has been identified. To do this, anticipated

labour and material costs should be estimated and compared with the sums recorded at the beginning of the exercise. The team should also estimate the cost of making the changes – new equipment, redundant stocks of existing materials, etc. – and deduct this from the overall saving. After the changes have been introduced, the team should follow up the results to confirm that its predictions have been realised. If they have not, then the reasons should be identified and appropriate action taken.

This brief description is intended only as a guide to the basic methodology of value analysis. Many refinements are possible which can be of great help when dealing with complex products.[5] Properly conducted VA exercises rarely produce disappointing results. Even on training courses, the savings achieved are usually at least 5% and often much more.

At one recent session in which the writer was involved, a team from a vehicle accessories firm analysed a motorist's footpump – a product subject to fierce competition, but very important in turnover terms to the firm. A production cost saving of 14% and a marked improvement in appearance were achieved through VA by the three-man team. The firm was delighted because a 'loss leader' had been turned into a 'usefully profitable line' once again. Only one member of the team was a designer. He felt that the presence of his two non-design colleagues and the intensity of the exercise had led to better, quicker results than he could have achieved working alone or with other design specialists. Several hundred thousand units of this product were being made by the firm each year, so that the total cost saving was substantial, even though the unit selling price was low. From a financial point of view, high volume products like this are usually the best choice as subjects for VA, because even slight cost savings are multiplied into respectable totals. However, low-volume products can yield attractive results where the unit selling price is substantial, where lack of any recent design review suggests generous scope for improvement, or where the priority is design improvement rather than cost reduction.

Sometimes cost–savings may be dramatically large and might suggest that earlier design work has been poor. Usually this is not the case. Often products are designed in prototype form using methods appropriate to 'one-off' manufacture. As production levels increase, these methods may remain in the specification, unless the initiative is taken to review them. In many companies, it is not clear whose responsibility this is, and so no changes occur until some kind of problem forces the issue. Similarly, a product may be deliberately designed to take advantage of under-utilised processes in the factory, although it is accepted that these may not be ideal. Unfortunately, as time passes and circumstances change, the need to switch to more economical processes is overlooked. Occasionally a VA exercise may reveal a safety hazard in the original design which can then be rectified before any injury occurs.

A programme of VA sessions is an excellent way for a firm to ensure that these kinds of problems are detected and solved instead of remaining hidden. Product designers are often well aware of deficiencies in designs, but may have little opportunity to influence changes once production is firmly established. Similarly, production departments and sales departments may well have strong views about the product's cost, appearance, quality, etc. yet may also feel frustrated through being unable to make a direct impact. VA brings together these interested parties and resolves very quickly what changes are possible and acceptable.

One other benefit of VA that should be mentioned is the change of attitude that participating employees often develop. They may feel able to identify with their firm's products in a new way. After all, they have directly influenced the design of the product which, therefore, is now partly their's. What is more, they may well have examined competitors' products during the exercise and will now be convinced (probably rightly) that their own product is best.

In view of all these advantages, why are some firms reluctant to use the VA approach? There seem to be two main reasons: The first is that some managers are suspicious of what they consider to be 'trendy' management techniques. They see VA as yet another gimmick likely to be irrelevant to their daily management activities. In fact, when exposed to a VA exercise and its cash saving results the reaction of managers is usually that they wish they had discovered the technique much sooner.

The terminology 'value analysis' may be partly to blame for the technique's lack of widespread use. Something more direct such as 'product cost review' or 'design review' would be more readily understood, but a term like 'design review' raises the problem that few companies like to admit that their product designs need any improvement. Often, cost savings are assumed to lie elsewhere – for example, in overhead costs, transport costs, or machine downtime. Similarly, the design of the product may be thought of as the rock upon which the company is based; great effort went into producing it and therefore changes cannot be lightly undertaken. However, existing designs must never be regarded as inviolable. Not many firms can afford to ignore cost savings of ten or twenty per cent and no firm should ever reject the opportunity to give its customers an even better product.

## 9.4 Evaluation of Design

Discussions about undertaking reviews of design, and using value analysis or other methods to achieve improvements, presuppose that it has been possible to evaluate the existing design with some degree of accuracy so that these improvements can be measured. Unless it is possible to compare the 'before and after' positions with confidence, work on design improvements cannot be carried out with any certainty that the right problems are being tackled.

Technical aspects of design present relatively few problems; most characteristics can be either measured directly or objectively assessed in some other way. Taking a motor car as an example, the performance of component parts such as the engine, transmission and braking system can be described using standard well-understood terms. In the case of the engine these would be power range, torque output, fuel consumption, wear rates, friction losses, etc; any consequences arising out of the use of a new material, a change in the shape of the combustion chamber, or the adoption of a new manufacturing process (for instance) could be readily evaluated in quantitative terms and the advisability of proceeding easily determined. Similarly, the technical design features of one product may be directly compared with those of competitors.

Ergonomic and economic aspects of products also lend themselves to this kind of objective measurement, although an element of subjectivity may have to be allowed for. For example, in the case of ergonomic features such as 'readability' of instruments, personal taste or opinion may influence judgements – preference for analogue or digital displays is a case in point. However, even here, experimental observations can supply valuable evidence to assist in making an overall evaluation. In most cases, the real problem is not encountered until the artistic or aesthetic aspects of a product are considered. An appraisal of the aesthetic elements cannot be carried out in the same objective way as an assessment of the other features. There are no universally recognised measures of attributes such as shape, style, colour and so on. Many managers readily admit to having little knowledge about these matters and often find difficulty when trying to explain why the appearance of one product is better than another. If they are honest, some designers will also admit a personal difficulty on this score. Only rarely can they point to some well-accepted principle of design which has been incorporated in the product and therefore makes it better. Sometimes they can apply their experience and training to deduce reasons why a design might be better but often it is the depth of their first-hand knowledge of current design trends or fashions which is their major contribution especially when dealing with mass-produced goods.

Taking the motor car as an example once again, most people would find it very difficult to evaluate, say, the 'front-end' styling of a selection of competing models. They would tend to express themselves using phrases such as 'model A looks cleaner than model B' or 'the shape of model A's headlamps is more modern than the other' and so on. The knowledgeable designer would know that aerodynamic studies or lighting technology might have had some influence on these points of styling and that current tastes are also important – perhaps economy-conscious motorists wanting cars which look sleek and energy saving.

The importance of fashion and evolving changes in taste should not be underestimated by companies. There is a tendency for some manufacturers to dismiss these things as unimportant with the result that their products may lose market share. Until recently this was certainly true of many British motor cars; it is also true of the few British radios which are still produced. They retain the unchanged styling of the 1960s, while foreign competitors have detected and exploited preferences for military-style, personal-style and so on.

Difficult as the evaluation of aesthetic design may be, it is still necessary to attempt it. It is also essential that design evaluation in general takes into account the impact of proposed changes upon customers. What designers or managers may know or believe to be important is of no consequence unless it is also a true reflection of customers' priorities.

One approach that can be used for evaluating all aspects of design across a sample of competing products is a simple ranking method. Ideally this should be carried out using a group of assessors including representatives of a cross-section of the consumers of the products. When the evaluation exercise is organised as a prelude to value analysis, then the VA team members can act as assessors. The first task is to draw up a list of attributes within each of the broad categories of design. Thus, using the heading 'technical design' would be listed all those aspects relating to function, operation, performance etc. Similarly for economic, ergonomic and aesthetic aspects of design. As already discussed, it is in this last category that most difficulty may be encountered and it is probable that the assessors will have to think hard to identify the attributes and how to describe them; professional designers specialising in the field should be consulted. Continuing the example of the motor car, part of a list of aesthetic attributes might look like this:

- Range of body colours.
- Topicality of colours.
- Range of interior finishes.
- Colours of interior.
- Material patterns used for interior.
- Harmonisation of interior and exterior colour schemes.

And so on until a list of perhaps several hundred attributes is achieved.

The next step is to assemble together examples of the product under investigation together with its direct competitors. Then armed with the complete list of attributes each assessor is asked (a) to place the products in order of rank against each attribute and (b) to give an opinion about the importance of each attribute, using a simple guide such as 0=Not important, 1=Fairly important, 2=Very important. The verdict of each assessor may be simply presented as follows:

| Attribute | Importance | Rank:Product | A | B | C | D |
|---|---|---|---|---|---|---|
| Colour range | 2 | | 2 | 3 | 1 | 4 |
| Interior finish | 1 | | 1 | 4 | 2 | 3 |
| Etc. | etc. | | etc. | | | |

This work should be done by each person working alone, but be followed by one or more group sessions to thrash out a consensus view. This may be very difficult and additional expert advice may be needed to reconcile wide differences of opinion. Finally, the resulting consensus view should be split into three parts according to the 0/1/2 importance scores. The '0' list may be set aside since these attributes have been judged to be of no importance. The '2' list be should given highest priority and within this those attributes against which the firm's own product received a low ranking should be earmarked for the most immediate attention during the subsequent re-design exercise.

It is quite easy to take the evaluation one step further and to convert each ranking into a score, perhaps giving a score of 10 points for a first place, 9 for second, and so on. Then multiplying each score by the importance weighting, an overall total score can be calculated for each product. If this whole evaluation is repeated at the end of the re-design exercise and a new score is worked out, the extent of the improvement may be judged. However, playing about with numbers in this way can be misleading if sight is lost of the fact that the evaluation is basically a qualitative exercise and that the introduction of a quantitative element is essentially to help identify the magnitude of any weakness or strength. The main benefit of such an evaluation is in identifying the aspects of the design which should receive greatest attention.

Some readers will be unimpressed by an approach such as this; designers, in particular, may feel that it trivialises something which is complex, obscure and demanding of their special skills. Obviously the writer would not accept this point of view. Rather, he would point to examples where the approach has been used with great success. One such is the Japanese manufacturer of vehicle seating which sent its representatives out to purchase examples of vehicle seats from every significant market in the world. Evaluation of the type described above was then carried out and each of the company's products was re-designed so that it suited the characteristics of the various markets better than all competitors' products including locally produced equipment.

The biggest danger in using this kind of evaluation procedure is that it will be approached in a mechanical way and that the results will be viewed with greater accuracy than they actually merit. In particular, it must be remembered that comparing existing products may tell more about the historical evolution of a category of design than about present and future trends. Before rushing into a re-design exercise to emulate the best features of competitors' current products, managers should pause to think about the lines that other companies may be pursuing for future products. Once again, specialist design knowledge should be sought to help in the product planning process.

Finally, whilst this section has been concerned with the evaluation of product design, it is also important that companies should evaluate each major design exercise to ensure that objectives are achieved and that value for money is received. This activity has been discussed in earlier chapters under the heading of 'design audits'; the product evaluation is an essential part of any design audit.

## 9.5 Conclusion

In looking at the need periodically to update product designs, this chapter has concentrated on the technique of value analysis. VA is controversial because it uses 'amateurs' in the design process and some design specialists dislike working in such a way. However, experience of VA exercises shows that excellent results may be achieved not only in terms of improved products, but also in other ways such as greater employee commitment and improved morale.

The importance of evaluating design was discussed and a method was presented which could be used by managers and others who lack specialist knowledge about design. With the warning that the method should be supported by qualified advice to identify trends, it was suggested that many firms would benefit from obtaining a clear understanding of their products through such an evaluation.

# 10 New Challenges for Design Managers

## 10.1 Introduction

Throughout this book, the aim has been to give an understanding of the range of problems and tasks which are associated with design activities. In order to produce something which is helpful to a wide range of companies and managers, most topics have been selected because experience has proved them to be common to many different design situations. This final chapter is about issues which will be of immediate concern only to a few companies, although eventually all companies which design products may need to take account of them. Specifically, it looks at computer aided design and attempts to give guidance about its applicability and use. It also considers the 'internationalisation' of design together with the trend to cross-national design groups.

## 10.2 Design and Computers

Computer aided design (CAD) is by no means a new phenomenom. Computers have been used in industry since the 1950s and from the earliest days they have been used in design offices as a means of improving efficiency, for example by performing routine calculations and simulations to test proposed solutions. However, it is only recently that CAD equipment has become easily accessible to designers and managers; previously the equipment has been either experimental in nature or part of a central company installation, in both cases usually available for operation only by specialist computer staff.

   The introduction of powerful mini- and micro-computers is now making

CAD available to a much wider range of potential users, although it is clear from the development work which is going on that the 'state of the art', particularly with respect to software, is still considerably behind that of other areas of business such as accounting, inventory or production control. It is normally necessary to develop CAD software for each individual company or application; standard programmes are not as useful as in other fields because of the extreme diversity of design activities in different companies. Some areas are better catered for than others, for example circuit design, process plant design, and building design, where there is a high degree of standardisation and repetition.

However, most programmes are devised for individual companies which are unlikely to be eager to share with competitors the productivity gains which well-managed CAD can achieve. Hence it is likely that the trend to custom-designed software will continue with its inherent high cost. This means that managers must weigh very carefully the benefits of CAD against the costs of adoption and development. They need to know whether their design activity (or part of it) is a suitable candidate for CAD and if so, what level of commitment is appropriate. Some guidelines are given in the next section.

The hardware associated with CAD needs to be mentioned at this point. The heart of a CAD system is usually a standard, multi-purpose computer which has a fast operating speed and is capable of handling large quantities of information. In bigger companies, a suitable computer may already exist which, if other activities permit, may be brought into CAD operations by the addition of appropriate input/output equipment. This additional equipment includes:

**Input**
 - A keyboard by means of which words, numbers and commands may be transmitted. The keyboard may also incorporate a number of 'function' buttons (or these may be separate) which are programmed to enter pre-determined commands.
 - An electronic 'tablet' which is divided into segments from which commands or data may be transferred to the computer by means of a special 'pen'. The data available via the tablet is identified by a 'menu' which is printed over the tablet.

**Output**
  – One or more visual display units upon which line drawings and numerical/verbal information may be presented.
  – A plotter or printer for producing drawings or parts lists.

This equipment is usually grouped together to form a work station (except the plotter which may be shared by several stations) and four or more stations may work with a single computer. Such a system would cost around fifteen times the employment cost of a senior draftsman, depending upon the type of plotter, data storage and software. A single station system based on a mini computer would cost around one third of this sum, while one of the more sophisticated micro computers could offer some facilities for a few thousand pounds.

## 10.3 Decisions about CAD

The indications of cost just given show that investing in CAD is still an expensive undertaking even for a single terminal mini-computer based system which is the minimum facility that would be useful to most industrially based design departments. Consequently, the decision to make this investment is an important one which must depend largely, though not exclusively, on the productivity improvements which are anticipated. In many applications to date, CAD equipment has been used primarily as a means of producing drawings more efficiently, and productivity gains of around 300% compared with manual drafting are typical.[1] Thus design departments which have to produce large quantities of manufacturing drawings (for example, manufacturers of special purpose or 'one-off' products) may well be able to justify the expenditure for this activity alone. However, really massive gains in productivity are only achievable when CAD equipment is used to actually design rather than simply to draw. Companies which are able to systematise the design process for their products and translate this into a programme, may enjoy productivity increases in design of several thousand per cent. The critical factor is the relationship between the effort and expense involved in creating each programme and the use to which it is put. Thus, company size may not be the crucial factor in decisions about CAD. A small company with a range of closely integrated products may be able to make more profitable use of CAD than a large company which manufactures many diverse products.

Each potential adoption of CAD needs to be assessed in the light of the maximum benefits that can be achieved and the *total* cost of the system that is being proposed. As in other computer applications, different systems (at different costs) are appropriate to particular situations. Whilst it may be perfectly feasible for the non-expert manager to make a preliminary appraisal of the case for introducing CAD the final decision should be made with the assistance of a consultant who is familar with the latest development in the field. Organisations which offer help to companies include the Computer Aided Design Centre in Cambridge and the Centre of Engineering Design at Cranfield. Individual computer companies and agents will also offer advice but, of course, are only likely to promote their own equipment which may not be the most suitable for a particular application.

Before deciding to adopt CAD, managers should first ask themselves the following key questions and if the answer to most or all of them is 'yes', then there is a strong chance that CAD can be used to advantage.

- Is a high proportion of design time spent on routine tasks, particularly in making drawings or attending to modifications?
- Does your company produce 'one-offs' which are essentially standard products scaled up or down, and perhaps modified, to suit the needs of individual customers?
- Is it important in your business to give quick responses to enquiries from customers? Does the preparation of these responses at present occupy too much of your designer's time?
- Would a reduction in design time (and hence the total time between receiving an order and making delivery) give your company an advantage over your competitors?
- Is there a shortage of skilled design staff in your special field?

Even where these conditions do not apply, there may still be a case for deploying CAD equipment. One example is where a company makes use of computer equipment in manufacturing (CAM) and the possibility arises of linking together the design and manufacturing stages. In an integrated CAD/CAM system, components can be designed and manufactured without the need to work from drawings – although these may still be produced – machining instructions, a bill of materials and a manufacturing programme can be all generated automatically.[2]

## 10.4 The Changing Role of Designers

The trends outlined in the last section imply substantial changes in the way that designers (and design managers) will work in the future. One of the beneficial results of an increased adoption of CAD is that a close working relationship is encouraged between design, manufacturing and other functions. Because the length of design projects is shortened and activities become combined or absorbed, there is an increased awareness of the need to make appropriate inputs at the correct time. Also, the presence of CAD/ CAM systems in companies often leads to the simultaneous design and development of both the product and the process – jigs, tools, machining sequences, equipment schedules and batch schedules may all be determined as part of the single design process.

One inherent danger in all this is that these activites may become dominated by the engineers in production and design departments. It may be difficult to find opportunities to enable the members of the design team who are conversant with aesthetics or ergonomics to make an adequate contribution to the product. The result would be the old problem of designs which are efficient from a manufacturing point of view but inappropriate for the markets in which they are to be sold. It is interesting that a report[3] about one British firm which has pioneered the use of CAD, highlights this very point. In that company, the industrial designers occupy what is referred to as a 'pivotal' role in forming the bridge between the market and the design and production engineers. These designers are responsible for showing to the rest of the project team the new product as a whole – for defining and interpreting the product specification and then ensuring that it is followed throughout the design process.

For many companies, the use of industrial designers in this way would constitute a major change from normal practice, despite there being much support for the view that designers should be used as 'integrators' regardless of whether CAD is involved or not. One of the recurring themes of this book has been the belief that designers should be involved in the product development process right from the beginning, including the policy making stage, before any specification is prepared or any individual project is started.

The setting up of 'cross-national' design groups is another trend which reinforces the need for this coordinating role of designers. In order to achieve an economic scale of manufacturing, many international companies are concentrating the production of a standard model at a single location rather than providing a different product for each market. This approach is particularly noticeable in the vehicle and domestic appliance industries where a model is now often designed to sell throughout the world, not just in one country. The demands this places upon designers are considerable for a much wider range of tastes has to be investigated and satisfied, and international standards and regulations must be met. To meet these challenges, design groups may draw members from many different countries. Some very large companies are now setting-up centralised design headquarters from which the majority of their new products emerge. To avoid becoming isolated from the needs of diverse markets, designers must have constant interaction with them. In particular, it is rarely possible to design completely standardised products which will sell in every market for local conditions (eg. electrical voltage, ambient temperature etc.) may demand some concessions. Thus cross-national design projects must identify these variations and allow for them in the design of the product; 'modularised' design is becoming more important in this respect involving interchangeable plug-in sub-assemblies which allow 90% or more of the product to be kept standard.

These trends have important consequences for the management of design and the training of designers. Design managers face the prospect of having to organise larger, more diverse groups of people working on increasingly complex projects. The conflict between creative expression and necessary constraints is becoming ever more intense. The key to success is a disciplined, systematic approach to the management of design. The training of managers should reflect this by incorporating design as an indispensable element in management development programmes. The education of design students can no longer be considered adequate unless it includes coverage of the kinds of topics presented in this book. The result of developing creative and technical skills without providing knowledge of industrial practice and problems will be frustrated designers unable to contribute significantly to the organisations for which they work.

## 10.5 Conclusion

The challenge of CAD and of more complex design projects are just part of what must be tackled by managers and designers working together. In many companies, the most important problem to be overcome is still the simple recognition that competent design is so crucially important to success. Those who doubt this need only look around them to see the emphasis that is placed on design by the most successful companies. They should also consider recent history as summarised in *figure 10.1*. During the post–war years, increasing affluence first created a demand for products of all kinds; almost any company that could put a product on the market was able to sell it.

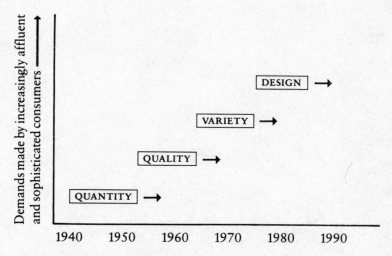

Figure 10.1 *Evolution of Consumer Demands and Level of Expectation*

Soon however, sufficient goods were on sale that customers could discriminate between the offerings of different companies; usually the deciding factor was quality. This caused manufacturers to react by providing new varieties of products. All the time customers were seeking higher levels of satisfaction. Now, in the 80's and probably through the 90's, many customers are viewing design as the main purchasing criteria. Knowledgeable customers recognise that many competing products now offer similar standards of quality and economic performance. Their decision to purchase boils down to choosing the product that looks best, works best and generally provides the greatest satisfaction. This is the challenge to be met by those who are managing product design.

# References

## Chapter 1

1 Gorb, P., 'Design Profitability and Organisational Outcomes', *Proceedings of the Design Policy Conference*, Royal College of Art, London 1982.
2 Lawrence, P., *Managers and Management in West Germany*, Croom Helm, 1980.
3 Pascale, R. T. and Athos, A. G., *The Art of Japanese Management*, Penguin, 1983.
4 Freeman, C., 'Design and British Economic Performance', Paper presented at the Royal College of Art, London 23 March 1983.
5 Moulton, A. E., *Engineering Design Education*, The Design Council, London 1976.
6 Carter, D., *Industrial Design Education in the United Kingdom*, The Design Council, London 1977.
7 Corfield, K. G., *Product Design*, National Economic Development Office, 1979.
8 Jones, J. C., *Design Methods*, John Wiley, 1980.
9 Topalian, A., *The Management of Design Projects*, Associated Business Press. London 1980.
10 Willock, J., 'The Design Triangle', *Designer*, April 1981.
11 Oakley, M. H. and Pawar, K. S., 'Managing Product Design in Small Firms', *Proceedings of the Design Policy Conference*, Royal College of Art. London 1982.
12 Lorenz, C. and Sieghart, M. A., 'Proving that quality takes some beating', Management Page, *Financial Times*, London, 12 January 1983.
13 *Facing International Competition*, Advisory Council for Applied Research and Development (ACARD). HMSO. 1982.
14 Osola, V. J., 'Innovative Response to a Changing World', *Proceedings of the Institution of Mechanical Engineers*, Vol 196, No 37, pp. 347–356, 1982.

## Chapter 2

1 Uytenhoeven, H. E. R., Ackerman, R. W. and Rosenblum, V. W., *Strategy and Organization: Text and Cases in General Management*, Irwin 1977.
2 Whitfield, P. R., *Creativity in Industry*, Pelican 1975.
3 Meadows, D. et al., *Limits to Growth*, Pan, 1972.

4  Prabhu, V. and Russell, J., 'The Truth About Production', *Management Today*, June 1979.
5  *Government Statistics – A Brief Guide To Sources*, HMSO (published annually).
6  *Profit from Facts*, HMSO (updated periodically).
7  *Guide to Official Statistics*, HMSO (updated periodically).
8  Skinner, R. N., *Launching New Products in Competitive Markets*, Associated Business Programmes 1974.
9  Midgley, D. M., *Innovation and New Product Marketing*, Croom Helm 1977.
10  Freeman, C., *The Economics of Industrial Innovation*, Penguin, 1974.
11  Wills, G. et al., *Technological Forecasting*, Penguin, 1972.
12  Twiss, B. C., *Managing Technological Innovation*, 2nd edition, Longman, 1980.
13  Wilson, A., *The Assessment of Industrial Markets*, Cassell Associated Business Programmes, 1973.
14  British Institute of Management, *Management Checklist Nos 29 & 30 – Launching New Products*, BIM London, 1977/79.
15  Holt, K., *Production Innovation: A Workbook for Management and Industry*, Newnes-Butterworth, 1977.
16  White, R., *Consumer Product Development*, Longman, 1973.
17  Blakstad, M., *The Risk Business*, The Design Council, London 1979.
18  Carson, J. W. and Rickards, T., *Industrial New Product Development*, Gower Press, 1980.

## Chapter 4

1  Farr, M., *Design Management*. Hodder and Stoughton, 1966.
2  Topalian, A., 'Designers as Directors.' *Designer*, February 1980.
3  Schon, D. A.,'The Fear of Innovation' in *Uncertainty in Research Management and New Product Development*, Ed. Hainer R. M. et al. Reinhold 1967.
4  Greiner, L. E., Patterns of Organisational Change, *Harvard Business Review* pp 119–130, May/June 1967.
5  *Innovation in Manufacture*, Institution of Production Engineers, London 1982.
6  Twiss, B. C., *Managing Technological Innovation*, 2nd edition, Longmans, 1980.
7  Lynton, R. P., Linking an Innovation Sub-system Into the System, *Administrative Science Quarterly*, pp 398–415, Sept 1969.
8  Bright, J. R., *Research, Development and Technological Innovation*, Irwin, 1964.
9  Roethlisberger, F. J. and Dickson, W. J., *Management and the Worker*, Harvard University Press, 1939.
10  Burns, T. and Stalker, G. M., *The Management of Innovation*, Tavistock Publications, 1966.
11  Whitfield, P. R., *Creativity in Industry*, Penguin, 1975.
12  Basil, D. C. and Cook, C. W., *The Management of Change*, McGraw-Hill, 1974.
13  Mueller, R. K., *The Innovation Ethic*, American Management Association, 1971.

14 Topalian, A., *The Management of Design Projects*, Associated Business Press, 1980.
15 Oldham, S. W., *Design and Design Management in the UK Footwear Industry*. The Design Council, London 1982.
16 Blakstad, M., *The Risk Business*, The Design Council, London 1979.

# Chapter 5

1 Weintraub, P. I., 'Big Business Goes Small', *Business Quarterly* (Canada), Vol 40, No 3, pp 48–55, 1975.
2 Ben Daniel, D. J., *The Technical Ventures Operations in Technology Transfer: Proceedings of the NATO Advanced Study Institute on Technology Transfer* (Eds Davidson H. F., Cetron M. J. & Goldhar J. D.), Noordhoff Publishing, Leiden, 1974.
3 Hannan, M., 'Corporate Growth Through Venture Management', *Harvard Business Review*. Vol 47, pp 43–61, 1969.
4 Gardner, J. B., 'Innovation through New Ventures: New Venture Concept in BOC', *R & D Management*, Vol 3, No 2, pp 87–89, 1973.
5 Vernon, A., 'A New Business Venture', *R & D Management*, Vol 4, No 2, pp 85–88, 1974.
6 Hill, R. M. & Hlavacek, J. D., 'The Venture Team: A New Concept in Marketing Organisation', *Journal of Marketing*, Vol 36, pp 44–50, 1972.
7 Burns, T. & Stalker, G. M., *The Management of Innovation* (2nd Ed.), Tavistock Publications, London 1966.
8 Stevens, H. A. R., 'Criteria for Selection of Venture Capital Projects', *R & D Management*, Vol 3, No 1, pp. 41–45, 1972.

# Chapter 6

1 White, R. R., 'Development Costs – A Law of Overspend'? in *Engineering Progress through Development*, Mechanical Engineering Publications, London 1978.
2 Corfield, K. G., *Product Design*, National Economic Development Office, London 1979.
3 Watts, P., *A Guide to the Preparation of Engineering Specifications*, The Design Council, London 1980.
4 Leslie, P., *Employing a Designer*, The Design Council, London 1980.
5 Jones, J. C. *Design Methods,* 2nd edition, John Wiley, 1980.
6 Mayall, W. H., *Principles in Design,* Design Council, London 1979.
7 Buck, C. H., *Problems of Product Design and Development*, Pergamon, 1963.
8 Leech, D. J., *Management of Engineering Design*, Wiley, 1972.

9  Buck, C. H. and Butler, D. M., *Economic Product Design*, Collins, 1970.
10  Oakley, M. H., 'Pencil in the Works', *Design*, Vol 408, December 1982.
11  Flurscheim, C., *Engineering Design Interfaces*, The Design Council, London 1977.
12  Blanco White, T. A., Jacob, R. and Davis, J. D., *Patents, Trade Marks, Copyright and Industrial Designs*, Sweet and Maxwell, 1978.
13  Johnston, D., *Design Protection*, The Design Council, London 1978.
14  *Applying for a Patent*, Patent Office, London 1978.
15  Myrants, G., *The Protection of Industrial Designs*, McGraw-Hill, 1977.
16  Miller, C. J. and Lovell, P. A., *Product Liability*, Butterworth, 1977.
17  Abbott, H., *Safe Enough to Sell?* The Design Council, 1980.
18  Abbott, H., 'How to Manage Liability', *Management Today*, July 1983.
19  *Facing International Competition*, Advisory Council for Applied Research and Development, HMSO, 1982.
20  Harding, H. A., *Production Management* (3rd edition). Macdonald and Evans, 1978.

# Chapter 7

1  Niebal, B. W. and Baldwin, E. N., *Designing for Production*. Richard D Irwin, 1957.
2  Parkinson, S. T., 'The Role of the User in Successful New Product Development,' *R & D Management*, Vol 12, No 3, pp 123–131, 1982.
3  Corfield, K. G., *Product Design*. National Economic Development Office, London 1979.
4  Stephenson, J. and Callander, R. A., *Engineering Design*, John Wiley, 1974.
5  Ross, I. M., *Effects of Organisational Procedures on Design – an outline of the problems in The Design Method* (ed Gregory, S. A), Butterworth, 1966.
6  Gallagher, M. J. and Welsch, L. P.,'Manufacturing', *Radio Corporation of America (RCA) Engineering*, Vol 2, No 4, pp 22–25 Dec–Jan 1975–76.
7  Turner, B. T., *Design Policy Formulation in The Design Method* (ed Gregory, S. A.) Butterworth, 1966.
8  Lock, D. L., *Project Management*, Gower Press, 1968.
9  Flurscheim, C. H., *Engineering Design Interfaces*, The Design Council, London 1977.
10  Watts, P., *A Guide to the Preparation of Engineering Specifications*, The Design Council, London 1980.
11  Mayall, W. H., *Sound Design Policies Sell Your Product*. Conference on Design Engineering and Management, Production Engineering Research Association (PERA), Melton Mowbray, 1966.
12  Brichta, A. M. and Sharp, P. E. M., *From Project to Production*, Macdonald, 1967.
13  Scott-Wilson, J. B., 'A Designer's Viewpoint of the Interface with Production, *Royal Aeronautical Society Symposium on Managing the Design/Production Interface*, London 1982.
14  Dangerfield, K. J. *Managing the Design/Production Interface*, Royal Aeronautical Society Symposium, London 1982.

15  Zarecor, W. D., 'High Technology Product Planning', *Harvard Business Review*, 1975.
16  Betts, D. J., 'Design for Production', *Business Management*, London, No 98, pp. 38–41, 53–54, 1969.

# Chapter 8

1   *Enterprise into the Eighties*. Confederation of British Industry, London 1979.
2   Amey, R. L., in Lever, H. and Edwards, G., (eds), *Banking on Britain*, Sunday Times Publications. London 1981.
3   Craver, J. K., 'Industrial Commercial Development', in Davidson, *H. F. Cetron*, M. J. and Goldhar, J. D., (eds), *Technology Transfer: Proceedings of the NATO Advanced Study Institute on Technology Transfer*, Noordhoff Publications, Leiden 1974.
4   Lawrence, P. R. and Lorsch, J. E., *Organisation and Environment: Managing Differentiation and Integration*, Division of Research, Harvard Business School, 1967.
5   Littler, D., 'Perspectives on In-company Technological Innovation,' *Design Studies*, Vol 1, No 6, pp 349–352, 1980.
6   Gisser, P., *Launching the New Industrial Product*, American Management Association, 1972.
7   Booz, Allen and Hamilton, Inc., *The Management of New Products*, 1968.
8   Gold, B., 'On the Adoption of Technological Innovations in Industry: Superficial Models and Complex Decision Processes', *OMEGA International Journal of Management Science*, Vol 8, No 5, pp 505–516, 1980.
9   Kolodney, R. and Pepino, G., 'Obstacles to Innovation', *European Business*, pp 14–18, October 1968.
10  Rothwell, R., 'Factors for Success in Industrial Innovation', *Journal of General Management*, Vol 2, No 2, pp 57–65, 1975.
11  Langrish, J., Gibbons, M., Evans, W. G. and Jevons, F. R., *Wealth from Knowledge*, Macmillan, 1972.
12  Topalian, A., *The Management of Design Projects*, Associated Business Press, 1980.
13  Parker, R. C., 'How Managements Innovate', *Management Today*, pp. 43–48, September 1978.
14  Parker, R. C., *Guidelines for Product Innovation*, British Institute of Management Foundation, London 1980.
15  Zarecor, W. D., 'High Technology Product Planning', *Harvard Business Review*, January/February 1975.
16  Harper, P. C., 'New Product Marketing: The Cutting Edge of Corporate Policy', *Journal of Marketing*, pp. 76–85, April 1976.
17  Datsko, J. 'Production Engineering Considerations in Product Design', *International Journal of Production Research*, Vol 16, No 3, pp 215–310, 1978

148 *Managing Product Design*

18 *Innovation and Competitiveness in Smaller Companies*. Confederation of British Industry, London 1979.
19 Child, J., 'Parkinson's Progress: Accounting for the Number of Specialists in Organisations', *Administrative Science Quarterly*, pp. 328–348, 1973.
20 Gregory, S. A. and Commander, M. W., 'New Materials Adoption Study: Some Contributions to Design Knowledge', *Design Studies*, Vol 1, No 2, pp 107–112, 1979.
21 Moody, S., 'The Role of Industrial Design in Technological Innovation', *Design Studies*, Vol 1, No 6, pp 329–339, 1980.

# Chapter 9

1 Buck, C. H. and Butler, D. M., *Economic Product Design,* Collins, 1970.
2 Miles, L. D., *Techniques of Value Analysis and Engineering* (2nd Edn). McGraw-Hill, 1972.
3 Gage, W. L., *Value Analysis*. McGraw-Hill, 1967.
4 Crum, L. W., *Value Engineering*. Longman, 1971.
5 Raven, A. D., *Profit Improvement by Value Analysis, Value Engineering and Purchase Price Analysis,* Cassell, 1971.

# Chapter 10

1 Gott, B. 'Why Can't We Manage CAD?' *Proceedings of Conference on Managing Computer Aided Design*, Institution of Mechanical Engineers, London 1980.
2 Smith, W. A. (Ed), *A Guide to CADCAM,* Institution of Production Engineers, London 1983.
3 Mazur, L., 'Baker Perkins' High-Tech Take-Up', *Management Today*, June 1983.

# Additional reading

Adams, J. L., *Conceptual Blockbusting: A Guide to Better Ideas*, Norton, 1980.
Bayley, S., *In Good Shape – Style in Industrial Products, 1900–1960*, The Design Council, London 1979.
Buggie, F. D., *New Product Development Strategies*, AMACOM, 1981.
Cafarelli, E. J., *Developing New Products and Repositioning Mature Brands*, John Wiley, 1980.
Cardozo, R. N., *Product Policy*, Addison Wesley, 1979.
Crawford, C. M., *New Products Management*, Irwin, 1983.
*Design and the Economy*, The Design Council, London 1983.
Dunne, P. and Obenhouse, S., *Product Management: A Reader*, American Marketing Association, 1980.
Farr, M., *Control Systems in Industrial Design*, Gower Press, 1973.
Johnson, G. and Scholes, K., *Exploring Corporate Strategy*, Prentice-Hall, 1984.
*Living by Design/Pentagram*, Lund Humphries, 1979.
*New Product Management for the 1980s*, Booz, Allen and Hamilton, Inc., 1982.
Olins, W., *The Corporate Personality – An Enquiry into the Nature of Corporate Identity*, The Design Council, London 1978.
Pessemier, E. A., *Product Management: Strategy and Organisation*, 2nd Edn, John Wiley, 1982.
Ramo, S., *The Management of Innovative Technological Corporations*, John Wiley, 1980.
Urban, G. L. and Hauser, J. R., *Design and Marketing of New Products*, Prentice-Hall, 1980.

# Index